POSTING THE NOTICE WHICH LOCATED WALL STREET

(See the descriptive note in the List of Illustrations.)

THE STORY OF A STREET

A NARRATIVE HISTORY OF WALL STREET FROM 1644 TO 1908

BY

FREDERICK TREVOR HILL

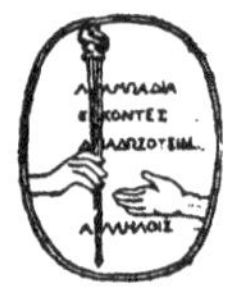

NEW YORK AND LONDON
HARPER & BROTHERS PUBLISHERS
MCMVIII

Published November, 1908.

TO

F. A. S.

CONTENTS

CONTENTS

ILLUSTRATIONS

ILLUSTRATIONS

ILLUSTRATIONS

ILLUSTRATIONS

ILLUSTRATIONS

FOREWORD

WALL STREET—the financial district—is an undefined territory of comparatively modern growth, teeming with news. Wall Street—the thoroughfare—is a narrow highway of comparatively ancient origin, crowded with history. Few streets in the world are entitled to equal fame. In the annals of American history it holds a place apart. Along its course the development of a great metropolis can be traced; within its confines originated much that concerned the founding of the nation; upon its stage many distinguished men and women played their parts. Its story is part of our national heritage.

Such is the tale that is told in these pages.

A few years ago it would have been well-nigh impossible to reconstruct this historic highway with any accuracy, or to depict the scenes enacted on it, or to repeople it with those who foregathered there, and to all the scholars and historians who have rendered this feasible the writer gratefully records his thanks, especially to the translators and compilers of the old Dutch and English records.

He likewise begs to express his appreciation to Mr. Samuel Palmer Griffin; Mr. Dingman Versteeg of the Holland Society; Mr. Wilberforce Eames of the Lenox Library; Mr. John D. Crimmins, and the officers and officials of the New York Historical Society, for the courteous assistance which they generously afforded.

October, 1908.

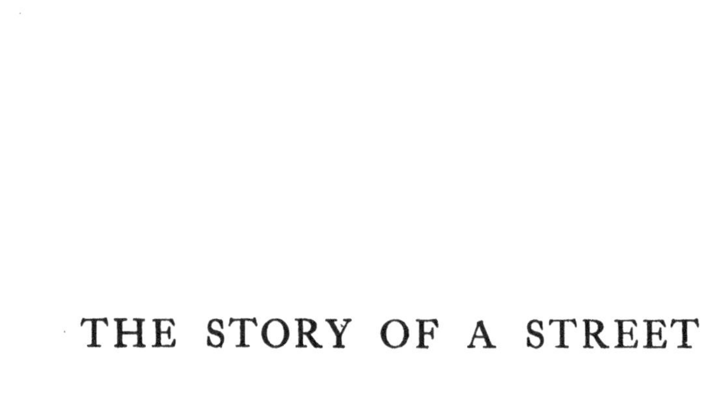

THE STORY OF A STREET

THE STORY OF A STREET

I

THE CATTLE GUARD

ON the morning of March 31, 1644, a man of clerkly appearance might have been seen standing at the entrance to the dilapidated fortress of New Amsterdam, with a sheaf of official papers in his hand. It was not an inviting prospect which confronted the observer that raw spring morning, for the roughly built, wooden houses scattered about the fort looked sadly weather-beaten, and the straggling, ill-made roads and paths which served as streets were littered with refuse and rubbish of every sort and ankle deep in mud. Even the new stone tavern on the East River and the still newer stone church, whose stanch construction had recently earned John and Richard Ogden a goodly builder's premium, appeared decidely bedraggled. Grimy mounds of melting snow encumbered each step of their stair-like gables, and the dirty water which trickled from them like muddy tears gave a finishing touch to their melancholy aspect. Nowhere was there a sign of cheer or comfort, and the unpaved streets were wellnigh deserted, save for a few disconsolate individuals who idled about the doorways, silently watching the hungry hogs rooting among the road refuse or exploring the muddy ramparts in search of food. To the north of the fort a badly placed windmill made a brave show of activity, groaning and whirring under the gusty winds from the bay, but its wild twistings to the capricious gyrations of the rusty weathercocks gave an air of futility to its exertions that was far from relieving the depressing desolation of the scene.

The man at the fort did not, however, waste much time in gazing at these discouraging surroundings. They were familiar to him in every dreary detail, for Cornelis Van Tienhoven had been Secretary of the Council at New Amsterdam for many years, and if he had ever been disturbed by the prevailing wretchedness of the town, it had long since ceased to afford him the slightest concern. Slowly turning his back to the view, he tacked one of his official documents to the wall of the fort, and then swinging about and picking his way across the miry ground to a convenient tree, affixed another paper. The few spectators of this proceeding viewed it with undisguised chagrin, for communications from the government were not apt to increase the happiness of the little Dutch settlement. On the contrary, they usually portended the imposition of some new burden or the curtailment of some coveted privilege at the hands of his High Mightiness, Governor Willem Kieft, whose six years of misrule had taught New Amsterdam to regard his proclamations with unmitigated dread. Unwelcome as they were, however, experience had taught the inhabitants that it was not prudent to ignore them, and the Secretary had scarcely posted his notices before people began to saunter from their houses and gather about the improvised bulletin-boards, the scholar in each group deciphering the script.

Van Tienhoven's handwriting was easily read. Indeed, good penmanship was the only qualification he had ever displayed for his office, and that virtue had wholly failed to endear him to the populace, who hated the very sight of his clerical fist. The particular notice he had transcribed that morning, however, was singularly free of offence. It merely recited a resolution of the Director and Council of New Netherland [1] that a barrier be erected at the north of the settlement, sufficiently strong to prevent the straying of cattle and to protect them from the Indians, and "warned" all interested persons to appear on "next Monday, the 4th of April, at 7 o'clock," for the prosecution of this work. A more reasonable demand probably never emanated from the Director-General, and yet it unquestionably suggested the belated closing of a stable door. During the administration of his predecessor, Van Twiller, almost all the cattle of the colony had mysteriously disappeared, and, as the ex-Governor's recently acquired bouwerie was found surprisingly well supplied with live-stock, there

[1] New York Colonial MSS. 4: 186. State Library, Albany.

were grounds for suspecting that some of the missing herds might have strayed in his direction. Kieft, however, was the last man in the world to investigate a trail of this sort, for there was honor among governors in those days, and William the Testy, though philosophic in no other respect, thoroughly believed in taking things as he found them. Indeed, rumor had it that his adherence to this belief was responsible for his migration from Holland, with his portrait adorning the public gallows to evidence his bankruptcy, and a charge of embezzling trust funds hanging over his head. These stories may have been the invention of enemies, but there certainly had been nothing in his conduct as governor to discredit them, and for dastardly cowardice and wanton cruelty his record had been unsurpassed. Indeed, it was a close question whether the Indians or the Dutch had the best cause for hating this representative of the Chartered West India Company in 1644; but, however that may have been, both feared him equally and lost no time in obeying his decrees.

It was not long, therefore, before the colonists were hard at work at the projected cattle-guard, and within a few days it stood completed. There is no authoritative information as to how it was constructed, but there is evidence that it consisted mainly of untrimmed trees felled at the edge of the adjoining forest and piled together to form a sort of barricade, and that its northern line, running certainly from the present William Street, New York City, to what is now Broadway, and possibly from shore to shore, marked the farthest limits of New Amsterdam, as it then existed, and practically determined the location of Wall Street.

Such was the origin of the best-known thoroughfare of the Western Hemisphere, and the same forest which supplied material for its earliest landmark doubtless furnished Adrian Block [1] with timber for the good ship *Restless*—an appropriate name for the first vessel launched from Manhattan Island, and prophetically suggestive of its most historic highway.

[1] The discoverer of Block Island.

THE CATTLE GUARD OF 1644
(See the descriptive note in the List of Illustrations.)

II

IN TIME OF PEACE—

DIRECTOR-GENERAL KIEFT did not survive his clumsy cattle-pen, for some three years after its completion the colony was relieved of his presence by the arrival of a new governor, whose advent was attended with truly royal ceremonies, and whose bearing and person suggested the very height of majesty. But the residents of New Amsterdam soon discovered that this kingly personage who had descended upon them, splendidly attired in a velvet jacket with slashed sleeves, a broad, drooping white collar, magnificently slashed hose secured at the knee by a rich scarf tied in a knot, and a shoe adorned by a large, bravely colored rosette, had little of the aloofness characteristic of the wearers of imperial purple. Indeed, he had not been long upon the shores of his new domain before he was stumping over it on his silver-banded wooden leg, sticking his nose into all sorts of odd corners, and ordering a general house-cleaning in no uncertain tones. Tyrannical he undoubtedly was, but the sway of Pieter Stuyvesant was that of a benevolent despot, confident that he knew what his subjects needed better than they did themselves, and determined that they should have it whether they would or no, and under his domineering, paternal rule the condition of New Amsterdam gradually improved.

The southern end of Manhattan Island was then much narrower than it is to-day. Pearl Street was its eastern boundary, and only a few hundred feet of meadow land separated Broadway from the North River. Within these slender limits, and south of the so-called fence, there were, less than ten years after Stuyvesant landed, nearly two hundred houses, peopled by almost a thousand tenants, while seventeen well-defined streets were already plainly traceable, which, thanks to the energy of the choleric Governor, were fairly clean. The houses were for the most part crudely constructed of wood, but some of the more substantial boasted variously colored glazed brick laid in checker, and wrought-iron

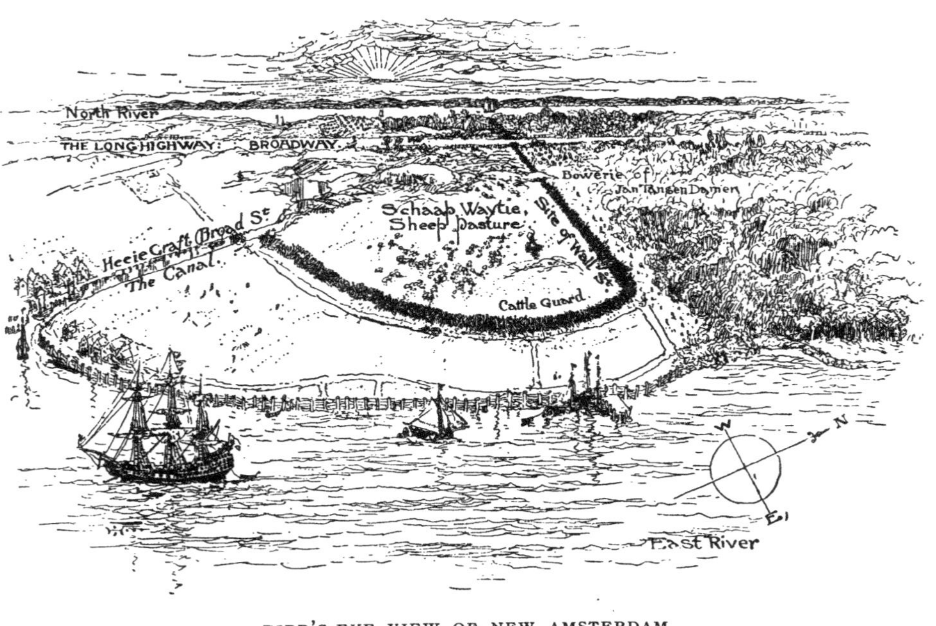

BIRD'S-EYE VIEW OF NEW AMSTERDAM
(See the descriptive note in the List of Illustrations.)

numerals to mark the date of construction, and even the humblest roof supported an ornamental weathercock. Moreover, nearly every house had a bright bit of garden, and if the general appearance of the little town was not as tidy as it has sometimes been pictured, it was not the fault of the tireless potentate who, from the moment of his arrival, ceaselessly harangued, scolded, bullied, and prayed for his people. Meanwhile the commerce of the community, which had been practically annihilated by Kieft's disastrous Indian wars, gradually revived, and for six peaceful years the wharf on the water-front witnessed an increasingly brisk business, wherein the natural instincts of the Dutch trader appeared to good advantage. Then news of hostilities between the United Provinces and England turned Stuyvesant's attention from civic affairs and brought into play his martial talents, concerning which authorities differ. But whether he was a hero or not at St. Martin, his wooden leg proves that he was at least at the post of danger, and he certainly rose to the occasion in 1653, when his country's possessions were threatened by the enemy. Indeed, he displayed such a bold front and such indomitable energy that he actually succeeded in inspiring the not too patriotic burghers of New Amsterdam with a little of his own spirit, and induced them to rush through some preparations for defence with really extraordinary speed. On March 13, 1653, the assembled burgomasters and schepens organized night and day patrols for guarding the approaches to the city; directed the skipper of the vessel representing the navy to bend his sails, load his pieces, and prepare for every emergency; recommended the repair of the fort, and resolved "to surround the greater part of the city with a high stockade and small breastwork to draw in time of need all the inhabitants behind it and defend as much as possible their persons and goods against attacks."

All this was accomplished at the morning session, and by the afternoon a goodly defence fund had been subscribed. Indeed, before two days had passed a committee of three was duly empowered to supervise the construction of the new works, and the members of this committee entered upon their duties with such energy that the following notice[1] was posted and cried within a few hours of their election:

> "NOTICE.—The committee appointed by the Director General, Council, and Magistrates of this city will receive proposals for a certain piece of work to set off the city with palisades twelve to thirteen feet long, by the rod. Any one who wishes to undertake this work may come to the City Hall next Tuesday afternoon, hear the conditions, and look over the work. Done, &c., Mch. 15, 1653.
>
> "Let one tell it to another."

Meanwhile, Stuyvesant was stumping along the line of Kieft's old cattle-guard, seeking an advantageous location for the palisade, and a brave picture the old war-dog must have presented as, splendidly attired, with sword at thigh and hand on hilt, he surveyed the ground and advised his bustling committee to erect the new defences some forty or fifty feet south of the old barrier and practically parallel to it—which advice, being accepted, determined the southerly line of Wall Street.

[1] *Records of New Amsterdam*, vol. i., p. 69.

III

THE PALISADE

ACTIVE as Committeemen La Montagne, Beeckman, and Wolfertsen (Van Couwenhoven) were, they could not immediately publish their plans, but before the day appointed for receiving bids the competitors for the contract were supplied with detailed specifications whose minuteness left nothing to be desired. The contemplated palisade was to be one hundred and eighty rods, or two thousand three hundred and forty feet, in length, extending from the East River (Pearl Street) straight across the island, skirting De Heere Graft (the ominously named canal which became Broad Street), and passing directly through what is now Trinity Church to a rise in the ground near the North River which afforded a natural breastwork. It was to be constructed of round wooden posts, twelve feet in length and eighteen inches in girth, sharpened to a point at the top, and placed in a line interrupted at intervals by larger posts, to which split rails were to be nailed two feet below the top. A sloping breastwork, a ditch, and a parade-ground were also contemplated, and lest all the minute par-

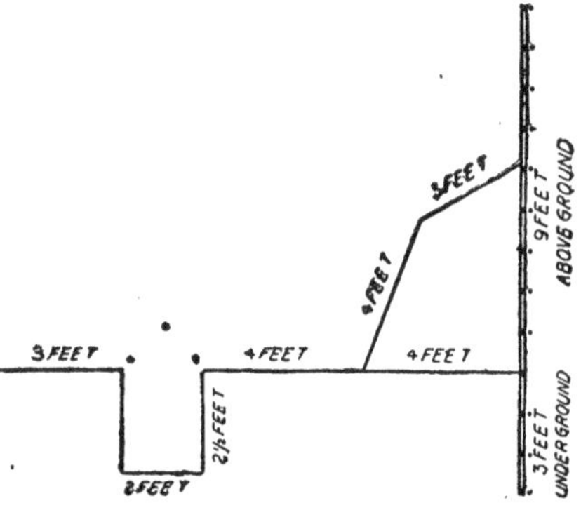

ticulars which the careful committeemen set forth should not suffice, they drew the above plan of the whole work and spread it upon the records of the burgomasters and schepens, where it remains to-day, an abiding memorial of their thoroughness and zeal.[1]

The bidding on these proposals was most en-

[1] *Records of New Amsterdam*, vol. i., p. 72.

couragingly brisk, no less than four competitors entering the lists, the successful candidate being Tomas Bacxter, whose subsequent career as a pirate may, as has been suggested, have been inspired by his success in securing this award. But however that may have been, we know from the official records that he was paid in "good" wampum (then coin of the realm),[1] and that the the cost was divided as follows:

1404 planks (@ 1½ florins)	2106	florins
340 posts	304	"
Nails	100	"
Transport	120	"
For setting them up and carpenters' wages.	500	"

or a total of about $1300, from which it would appear that "setting them up" was even then an important item in the estimates of municipal contractors. Bacxter completed his work in about six weeks; but no enemy having appeared to test its powers of resistance, the enthusiasm of the burgomasters and schepens speedily

[1] The value of wampum, or "devil's currency," depended upon quality, and was regulated by law. (Ordinance of May 30, 1650.)

WALL STREET IN 1653
(See the descriptive note in the List of Illustrations.)

waned, and in spite of Stuyvesant's urgent remonstrances the repairs to the fort remained wholly neglected. Indeed, when the question of paying for the palisade, breastwork, and ditch was presented to their worships, they stoutly declared that the West India Company was bound to defend its own property without expense to the citizens, and from this position they would not recede until Stuyvesant abandoned the excise duties imposed upon the inhabitants and surrendered to the civic treasury the revenue derived from that source. This masterly stroke of business was undoubtedly Wall Street's first financial triumph.

About two years after this event Stuyvesant's raid against the Swedish settlements on the Delaware, and the attacks of the Indians at Hoboken, Pavonia, and Staten Island, caused the city fathers to look again to their defences, for it had been discovered that some sixty-five of the palisades had been chopped down for firewood, and that the whole work had otherwise fallen into such a sad state of repair that extensive renovations had become imperative. Probably it was at this date that the five bastions shown on what is known as the "Duke's Plan" [1] were constructed. These were small, two-gun artillery mounts, one of which projected from the wooden bulwark at what is now the head of Hanover Street; another covered the present site of No. 44 Wall Street, just west of William Street; a third stood on part of the ground now occupied by the Sub-Treasury; a fourth dominated No. 4 Wall Street; and the last commanded what was to become Trinity church-yard, from a point a little to the rear of the existing church.[2] In addition to these formidable batteries, the defences were further strengthened by nailing boards to the height of ten or twelve feet above the sharpened ends of the palisades, forming a sort of screen calculated to prevent the Indians from scaling the barricade; but as no enemy appeared, the war-like energies of the burghers again subsided, and before long two gateways were constructed to facilitate communication between the townspeople and the farmers of the outlying bouweries. One of these openings, known as the Land Gate, was situated at Broadway, and the other, called the

[1] See copy in possession of New York Historical Society.
[2] Innes' *New Amsterdam and its People*, p. 272.

THE-WATER GATE, FOOT OF WALL STREET, 1679
(See the descriptive note in the List of Illustrations.)

Water Poort, pierced the stockade at what was then the river road (now Pearl Street),[1] and for nine more or less peaceful years a steadily increasing stream of commerce poured through these narrow apertures. Then rumors of war once more caused them to be closed and barricaded.

Again, as in 1653, it was the English who threatened, although no war had been declared, and again Stuyvesant succeeded in diverting the inhabitants from the joys of successful trading to the less profitable duties of patriotism. From August 29, 1664, to September 2, the vigorous Governor, then seventy-two years of age, hopped and hobbled anxiously up and down the length of the palisade, encouraging and berating the workers tinkering at the defences under a hot summer sun; but patriotism was sadly lacking, and most of the labor was performed by negro slaves whose masters begrudged their services. Indeed, there was something pathetic about this

[1] About this time (1655–56) the residents of Pearl Street, inconvenienced by the high tides, caused a sea-wall to be erected, and the space between this barrier and their houses to be filled in, making a roadway known as De Waal, or Lang de Waal. Incautious investigators have confused this with Wall Street, and their error has resulted in some astonishing "history."

final effort of the gallant old martinet to rouse the citizens to resistance, and those who have the right sort of eyes and ears properly attuned maintain that his shadow can still be seen o' nights striding defiantly through Wall Street, anxiously inspecting the vanished works, and that the sound of his cane and his silver-shod stump can be heard echoing through the deep cañon of brick and stone.

Unsupported as he was, however, Stuyvesant managed to keep his unwilling workers at their task until news reached the city that the Duke of York's war-vessels were in the harbor and that their commanders offered liberal terms for immediate surrender. Then the intrenching tools were thrown aside, and despite the Governor's prayers and remonstrances the populace virtually welcomed the invaders. Doubtless resistance would have been futile, and submission to the semi-piratical attack was the part of prudence, but the lonely figure of the grim Dutch warrior, standing gamely by his guns, will always contrast gratefully with the crowd of discreet traders gaping at the enemy from Battery Park, and make one doubt the maxim defining the better part of valor.

IV

PIONEER PROPRIETORS

THE town which thus easily fell into the hands of that royal buccaneer, the Duke of York, had grown during Stuyvesant's administration. In it the new Governor, Colonel Richard Nicolls, found no less than two hundred and twenty houses and over fourteen hundred people, while facing the parade-ground, designed for the manœuvring of troops behind the palisade, there were at least ten dwellings occupied by a merchant trader, a wool spinner, a chimney-sweep, a tapster, a miller, and other estimable citizens of a similar class. Indeed, the house of the merchant trader — one Moesman — had been erected as early as 1656 on a portion of the site lately abandoned by the Custom House,[1] and was presumably the first residence known to Wall Street.

[1] Now National City Bank Building.

Nicolls attempted no disturbing innovations in the administration of the city which then became New York, and it is doubtful if he was responsible for the alterations in the palisade which were made in the year of the surrender. However, four of its five original bastions disappeared about that time, the one on the present site of No. 44 Wall Street alone remaining as first placed, and the so-called fortification continued in practically this condition for nine years, when the city passed, without a struggle, into the possession of its former owners.

This time the capture was effected in time of war, Admirals Evertsen and Benckes quietly sailing into the harbor during the absence of Governor Lovelace, and landing Captain Anthony Colvé at about the foot of the present Park Place to take possession of the city and establish martial law. Almost the first act of this military governor was to demolish some buildings which had been erected just outside the palisade, the western line of which he then proceeded to rebuild, turning it to the south almost along the present site of Rector Street. He also forbade all entrance to or exit from the city except through

THE ALLAERDT VIEW OF NEW YORK, CIRCA 1668
(See the descriptive note in the List of Illustrations.)

the gates[1] under penalty of death, and those avenues of communication were rigidly closed after nightfall. All this occurred before the spring of 1674, and within a twelvemonth the city once more reverted to England under the terms of peace with Holland.

The returning Englishmen found the city obviously larger than they left it, and steadily pressing upon the northern barrier. Fully seventeen houses now faced the parade-ground lying parallel to and immediately behind the palisade, its width of a hundred feet affording a sufficiently inviting frontage to induce the construction of at least one house of the first class, one of the second, and seven of the third, and giving promise of a generously broad thoroughfare—a promise destined to remain unfulfilled.

Meanwhile the palisade, which had long outlived its usefulness, was repeatedly repaired, and it was not until 1685 that the land immediately north of it became the subject of a notorious speculation which inflicted irreparable injury

[1] The bastions were known as "Hollandia" and "Zeelandia." The gates were at Broad Street and at "Smit's Vly." (Innes' *New Amsterdam and its People.*)

upon the future highway. His Excellency Thomas Dongan was the royal Governor at that time, and his sharp eyes, which rarely wandered from the main chance, quickly detected a business possibility in this property. Indeed, he was in a position where he could materially influence its value, and if he did not make the most of his opportunity it will have to be conceded that he did the best he knew. Through the agency of a "dummy" purchaser—one Captain John Knight of his official staff—he secretly acquired from the Damen estate a strip of land a thousand feet long and eighty feet deep fronting upon the wall,[1] together with all the right, title, and interest which the sellers had in the parade-ground behind the wall, which they and every one else supposed would become the public thoroughfare. The day after this deal had been safely consummated, however, Dongan ordered one Leonard Beckwith to survey the wall[2] and officially establish the new street, and so promptly did the surveyor set about his task that he returned a report within twenty-four hours, laying out a

[1] N. Y. Register's Office, L. 13, pp. 124–150, Dec. 14, 1685.
[2] *Manual of Common Council.* 1851: 406.

street not one hundred, but thirty-six, feet in breadth, and, presto! Dongan's eighty-foot lots became one hundred and twenty-four feet deep. By this financial coup the royal Governor achieved the distinction of being the first insider to make something out of nothing on the narrow, if not straight, path which resulted from his acquisitiveness.[1]

[1] Captain Knight took title by deed dated December 14, 1685; the warrant for Beckwith's survey is dated December 15, 1685; his survey was made December 16, 1685. Knight's deed to the Governor was apparently dated before he acquired title (March 9, 1685), but his Excellency did not record the instrument for three years. (*Manual of Common Council*, 1851, and records in New York Register's Office, L. 18, p. 64.)

V

CAPTAIN KIDD AND OTHER PIRATES

THREE years later Dongan again turned his attention to Wall Street, appointing commissioners to make an official inspection of the palisade and inform him as to its condition, the upshot of which was a report showing the Water Gate and the artillery mounts in ruins, the Land Gate tottering, the curtain palisades either prostrate or falling, and the land actually staked out for building purposes. Of this last fact, however, Dongan must have been even better informed than his commissioners, for he was then actively marketing some of his queerly acquired property, and by as strange a chain of circumstances as was ever unearthed from the records, one of his lots passed into the hands of a gentleman whose exploits have been recounted in verse and prose for more than two hundred years.

This historic parcel of land (part of which is

now known as No. 56 Wall Street) lies opposite the head of the present Hanover Street, and one Browne was the original purchaser. Browne almost immediately transferred his bargain to a well-known citizen named William Cox, whose wife Sarah (*née* Bradley) was destined to greater fame than he. Shortly after acquiring this plot Cox is said to have built a house upon it, and if this be so the building was the first erected on the north side of Wall Street. In 1689, however, he succumbed to what has since proved fatal to many dwellers on that highway, for the report of his demise says that he "took too much water in," and his widow, to whom he left his property, straightway consoled herself by marrying one John Oort. This gentleman fell a victim to her charms so speedily that she took out letters of administration on his estate, May 15, 1691, and the next day married no less a person than Captain William Kidd, the future pirate, who thus became one of the earliest proprietors of Wall Street — a locality in which people have been treasure-hunting for over a century.[1]

[1] Kidd's residence was on Pearl Street. He also owned 25–29 Pine (then Van Tienhoven) Street. After his death

But Captain Kidd was not the only pirate known to New York at the latter end of the seventeenth century. Indeed, the little city, with its rascally governors and its mixed population, many of whom were adventurous traders ready to turn almost any kind of penny, was for years a favorite stamping-ground of the sea-rovers, and their gorgeous persons became very familiar not only to Wall Street but throughout the whole town, where their confidential transactions with certain enterprising citizens laid the foundation of more than one existing fortune.

Meanwhile the palisade still survived, and if it be true that the English laughed when they first inspected it, they kept up the joke a long time, for in 1692—seven years after Dongan had had the street surveyed—it was once more repaired,

his much-married widow became the wife of Christopher Rousby, and she and her latest husband, fearing that Kidd's alleged piracy would work a forfeiture of his property, conveyed all the lands in which he had been interested to Viscount Cornbury, the then Governor, and received from him, in the name of Queen Anne, a deed giving them a title unclouded by Kidd's "enterprises."

For these facts and for tracing Kidd's ownership of 56 Wall Street the writer is indebted to Miss Jennie F. Macarthy, of the Title Guarantee and Trust Company of New York.

substantial stone bastions being erected on the site of the artillery mounts at William Street and at Broadway, and three years later, just after the street had been partially paved, more renovations were attempted.[1] Indeed, a contemporary historian remarked that the maintenance of this wall cost the community some £8000, and described it as "a monument to our Folly." Nevertheless, it was not until 1699 that a committee of citizens petitioned his Excellency through the Common Council to remove it as an obstructing nuisance and utilize the stones of its bastions for the new City Hall.[2]

Then the end came, and with the passing of this ancient landmark New York ceased to be a walled city, and its new highway almost immediately became the resort of so many noted men and the scene of such dramatic events that for wellnigh a hundred years its story supplies a unique foot-note to American history.

[1] *Minutes of Common Council*, vol. i., p. 412.
[2] *Ibid.*, vol. ii., p. 82.

VI

THE SHAPING OF THE STREET

HAD Captain Kidd revisited Wall Street some three-and-forty years after he had become one of its pioneer proprietors, he would have found himself in strange surroundings, and it is not at all probable that he would have realized the dignity or importance of the thoroughfare from any external evidence. Indeed, the street presented, in 1734, a decidedly ragged and unattractive aspect. At its eastern end, or Slip, in front of the Long Island Ferry, stood the flimsily constructed Meal Market, whose transactions in corn and similar merchandise had been supplemented by a more profitable traffic in negro slaves, who were daily displayed in its stands for the benefit of those desiring to buy, sell, or hire such commodities, and on either side of this unsavory mart stretched a broken line of mean little wooden buildings

BIRD'S-EYE VIEW OF WALL STREET ABOUT 1735

extending as far west as William Street. From this point the prospect gradually improved, the Broadway end boasting some dwellings of neat and attractive appearance, but the north side remained entirely vacant save for four wholly dissimilar structures. The first of these, on the northwest corner of William and Wall streets, was the property of Gabriel Thompson, a tavern-keeper, beyond which loomed a huge, barn-like affair erected by the Bayards in 1729, for what they termed "the mystery of sugar refining"—a mystery which Wall Street has not wholly fathomed to the present day — and adjoining this crude factory stood the most pretentious building on Manhattan Island—the City Hall—whose foundations had been laid in 1699 with the stones taken from the bastions of the old palisade. Beyond this, and almost adjoining it, lay the Presbyterian Church, a substantial brick edifice, and at the head of the street, on Broadway, squatted the ugly, square little wooden building with a disproportionately tall steeple which had sheltered the congregation of Trinity Church since 1696.

Such was the condition of the street which

had in less than half a century acquired political if not social ascendency over all other thoroughfares of the city which now boasted a population of nearly ten thousand souls. The most potent influence effecting this result had, of course, been the selection of the street as the site of the City Hall, for that building was not only the seat of government but the social centre, New York in those days being ruled by an aristocracy whose nod made the laws and set the fashions. The presence of Trinity Church had likewise given the street a certain social prestige, for it had almost immediately become the semi-official place of worship, with a pew reserved for the Mayor, Recorder, Aldermen, and other dignitaries, and its list of parishioners included many of the most notable people in the community. In fact, when Messrs. De Peyster and Bayard, who had purchased a large part of Governor Dongan's queerly acquired holdings of the northern frontage, enabled the Presbyterian Church to obtain a broad foothold, practically all the spiritual and temporal power of the city lay concentrated on the narrow, unlovely highway. Under these circumstances it is not at all surprising that

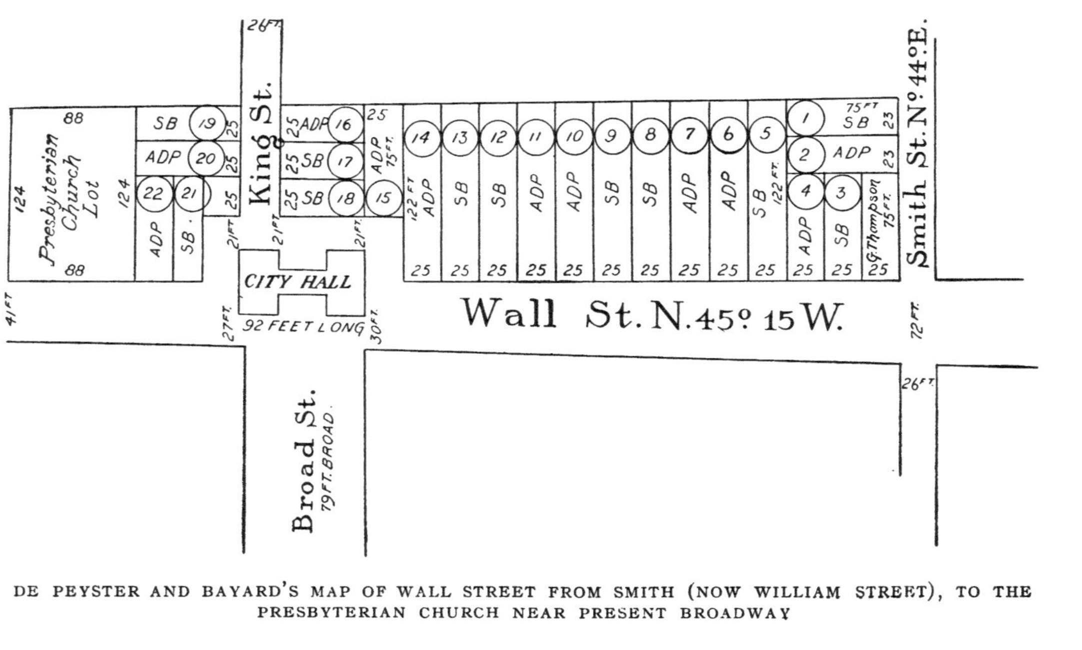

DE PEYSTER AND BAYARD'S MAP OF WALL STREET FROM SMITH (NOW WILLIAM STREET), TO THE PRESBYTERIAN CHURCH NEAR PRESENT BROADWAY

well-to-do families soon began to establish comfortable residences in proximity to the churches, that the mercantile and financial exchanges clustered along the site of the old canal to the very steps of the City Hall, and that that building became the scene of almost every event associated with the early history of the rising city.

As originally planned, the City Hall was far from a triumph of architecture, but it was dignified and spacious, affording accommodations for a court-room, a jury-room, the Common Council chamber, a jail, a library,[1] and a debtors' prison, to say nothing of space reserved for the Fire Department, whose water-supply was partially obtained from two Wall Street wells.[2] Severely simple as was the external appearance of this commodious building, it had cost no less than

[1] This library, the first known to New York, consisted of 1642 volumes indirectly bequeathed about 1728 by the Reverend John Millington, to which was added the collection of the Reverend John Sharp, the whole constituting the "Corporation Library," which eventually became the existing New York Society Library.

[2] One of these, known as Frederick Wessel's well, was located on Wall just west of William Street; the other lay between Broad and New streets. (*Old Wells and Water-courses of Manhattan*, by Waring and Hill.)

£4000, and the Earl of Bellomont regarded it as such a fitting monument to his administration that he caused his and the Lieutenant-Governor's coats of arms to be emblazoned on its walls. This solitary effort at ornamentation was, however, ruthlessly destroyed within a few years, when the Earl became unpopular, and no further attempt at adornment was made until 1715, when Stephen De Lancey erected at his own expense an elaborate cupola containing a clock with four substantial dials.[1]

Opposite the City Hall, and directly at the head of Broad Street, stood the cage,[2] pillory, stocks, and whipping-post, whose victims were daily in evidence, reminding the citizens of the

[1] "*Ordered*, That the committee do treat and agree with some proper person for the making of a public clock with four dyal plates."—*Minutes of the Common Council*, vol. iii., pp. 108, 136–7.

DeLancey received a vote of thanks for his gift, February 23, 1715.

[2] "Nov. 1, 1703. *Resolved*, That a cage, whipping-post, pillory, and stocks be forthwith erected before the City Hall."—*Minutes of the Common Council*, vol. ii., p. 244.

"Nov. 2, 1710. *Ordered*, That the cage, pillory, stocks, and whipping-post be removed to the upper side of Broad Street, a little below the City Hall."—*Minutes of the Common Council*, vol. ii., p. 425.

grim administration of the law at the seat of government. Indeed, Wall Street not infrequently witnessed other ugly forms of retributive justice, for offending slaves were often paraded up and down the highway, receiving a fixed number of lashes at every corner; and although there is no record of any execution having taken place in the street, the first trial of importance which occurred in the City Hall involved a charge of treason, the penalty for which was death.

The accused in this famous cause was Colonel Nicholas Bayard, and the proceedings demonstrated that New York had nothing to learn from the star-chamber methods of the mother-country, for no case was ever more tyrannously conducted from first to last than that which resulted in the conviction of the distinguished prisoner. Bayard was indicted on a flimsy charge based upon a petition criticising the government, and all the bitterness engendered by years of political strife found expression in his prosecution. Not only were the judges and the Attorney-General bent upon securing his conviction, but the jury was selected to insure this result—one of its members being related to the presiding justice and the others being almost equally disqualified. Under such circumstances a defence was practically futile, and amid a scene of great excitement, both within and without the court-room, a verdict of guilty was rendered and the prisoner promptly sentenced to die on the gallows. Wall Street, however, escaped witnessing this judicial murder, for a so-called confession was finally extorted from the condemned, who was then released, his discharge completing the mockery which politics had made of the law.

VII

AT THE WALL STREET PILLORY

DESPITE its acknowledged prestige and manifest advantages there was very little evidence of Wall Street's prosperity or popularity at high noon on November 6, 1734. Indeed, a more silent and deserted highway could scarcely be imagined. Not a coach rumbled up or down its cobbled road-bed, no pedestrians were astir, and its houses showed no sign of life. In fact, the whole street, from the water's edge to Trinity, appeared to be in the possession of two men who stood near the pillory, whipping-post, stocks, and cage at the head of Broad Street, opposite the City Hall. One of those lonely individuals, however, was a person of some consequence in the community whose presence betokened a public function of no ordinary importance, for Francis Harrison, the Recorder, was a dignified gentleman whose offices could be required only for affairs of state, and the paper which he proceeded to read in stentorian tones demonstrated that he was attending in his official capacity. For a time it seemed as though the worthy Recorder would have no auditor except the negro slave who stood at his elbow, but before he concluded a little group of officers sauntered up Broad Street from the direction of Fort George and paused to learn the occasion of this proclamation to an empty street. Solemn, indeed, was the occasion as disclosed by the Recorder, who with due form and ceremony recited an order of the Council, dated October 17, 1734, wherein and whereby it appeared that one John Peter Zenger had set up, printed, and published divers and sundry nefarious matters defamatory of the government and of His Excellency Governor Cosby in a news sheet or paper known as the *New York Weekly Journal;* wherefore it was decreed that certain issues of said paper, numbered 7, 47, 48, and 49,[1] should be burned near the pillory at the hands of the Common Hangman or Whipper as

[1] These and subsequent details are derived from a rare publication in possession of the New York Bar Association, entitled "Narrative of the Case and Trial of John Peter Zenger," issued in London in 1752.

a public warning to the writer and other evil-minded persons, and that the printer should be duly prosecuted for the injurious statements contained in his sheet. Very little of all this was sufficient to put the Recorder's slim audience in touch with the situation, for Governor Cosby's recent encounter with the local authorities over the case of the *Weekly Journal* was unpleasantly familiar to all the powers that were. Indeed, every one in town knew that His Excellency had overreached himself by ordering the Mayor and City Magistrates to attend the destruction of Zenger's paper, and that those functionaries, quick to resent an infringement of their liberties, had instantly denied his right to impose any such duty upon them, flatly refused to lend their presence to the scene, and forbidden their hangman to execute the Governor's decree. This angry clash of authority had been followed by a petition from the Sheriff praying that the public whipper be designated as the person to apply the torch, and when his request had been denied the coerced official had appointed a negro slave to act as his deputy, and the public had decided by common consent to support the local authorities by shunning the scene of action at the appointed hour.

Such was the explanation of Wall Street's deserted aspect, but Recorder Harrison was equal to the occasion, and the four offending papers were duly burned by the Sheriff's humble substitute, to the thorough satisfaction of the spectators, who gravely watched the flames until the last scrap was reduced to ashes and then turned on their heels, with an exchange of formal salutes, Harrison retiring to the City Hall and the officers to their local barracks.

It would be difficult to imagine a more childish performance than this whole proceeding, and even from a childish stand-point it was far from a success, for the fire was not a good one and its flames were poorly fed. Yet of this tiny blaze, started in Wall Street in the fall of 1734, came a mighty conflagration which wellnigh lit a world.

BURNING ZENGER'S "WEEKLY JOURNAL" IN WALL STREET, NOVEMBER 6, 1734

(See the descriptive note in the List of Illustrations.)

VIII

A FIGHT FOR FREEDOM OF THE PRESS

JOHN PETER ZENGER, whose editorial pages were thus cleansed with fire, was not the ablest journalist of New York, and Governor Cosby, whose administration he attacked, was not its worst Executive. The whole history of the city, however, had long been an inglorious recital of greed, corruption, incompetence, and arrogance, the royal governors having included a gentleman who made the seaport the most desirable of all piratical resorts; a noble personage who took pleasure in masquerading in woman's clothing and exhibiting himself in this guise, with the pleasing delusion that he might be mistaken for Queen Anne, and a solemn nonentity who took himself so seriously that he exacted more deference and reverence than would have been accorded to his royal master. In fact, all the powers that were, including the landed gentry and the personal and political favorites of the provincial court, displayed an undisguised contempt for the masses, affecting an elegance of attire in which dress swords, ruffled shirts, silk stockings, and short-clothes served to emphasize the class distinctions. Not all the members of this little aristocracy, however, were Englishmen, for no more proud or exclusive dignitaries ever strutted than the Dutch patroons; and when the ponderous travelling coach of one of those Lords of the Manor lumbered down Wall Street's cobbled roadway, on official business bent, there were few who disdained to court recognition, while the populace frankly stared with admiring wonder, many of them cap in hand.

It was this condition of affairs that had brought Zenger to the front as the nominal editor and publisher of the *Weekly Journal*, which had, as a matter of fact, been established and largely supported by James Alexander and William Smith, two able lawyers, under whose active leadership a popular party was rapidly forming.

Zenger himself was a young man of more

courage than education, whose boldest utterances read very mildly in these days of unbridled denunciation; but any criticism of official actions was then regarded as presumptuous, and his shafts evidently hit the mark, for the destruction of his pages had been planned as a most impressive ceremony, and the humiliating fiasco which had resulted virtually forced the government to take further proceedings in defence of its dignity. Some ten days later, therefore, Zenger was arrested at the instance of Governor Cosby and lodged in jail, where he remained for many months in default of excessive bail. Meanwhile the public began to take an unprecedented interest in the affair, and, under the energetic leadership of Alexander and Smith, such a strong sentiment was aroused in favor of the accused that the Grand Jury refused to find an indictment against him, and the Attorney-General was compelled to resort to extraordinary measures to prevent his release. This merely intensified the popular feeling, however, and before long all the scattered opponents of the government rallied to the slogan, "Freedom of the press!" and united in supporting the imprisoned editor, whose cause immediately became a political issue of far-reaching effect.

Never before had the general public been identified with any determined effort to secure freedom of the press in America, and far-seeing men throughout the country, including Benjamin Franklin and other aspiring journalists, watched the struggle with keen interest, while in New York the opening moves of Zenger's counsel resulted in such sensational developments that public excitement was kept at the highest pitch.

IX

THE TRIAL OF A CAUSE CÉLÈBRE

ZENGER had been confined in the City Hall, and it was here that the lawyers for the defence began the proceedings which were destined to assume historic importance. These public-spirited advocates were no other than Messrs. Alexander and Smith, under whose covert patronage the *Weekly Journal* had been founded, and their appearance in the cause was particularly obnoxious to the government, which rightly suspected them of having personally contributed some of its most offensive material. Moreover, only a few years earlier they had virtually abolished the Court of Exchequer expressly convened by Governor Cosby for the destruction of Rip Van Dam, a popular official, and to punish Chief-Justice Morris for his decision in that case the angry Executive had removed him and appointed James De Lancey in his place. De Lancey was a jurist of exceptionable ability, but a thorough partisan of the government, and Zenger's counsel had good reason to know that their client would receive very little consideration at his hands. Their first move, therefore, was to challenge his and the associate-justice's[1] right to sit upon the bench, and regardless of consequences the petition for their removal was presented to the very men they were seeking to depose. Both the Chief-Justice and his associate had been appointed during the pleasure of the Governor, and not during good behavior, and this illegality it was claimed absolutely disqualified them from holding court. There was no little shrewdness in thus appealing directly to De Lancey's sense of propriety, but it was too much to expect that a man of his character would scruple to judge his own case, and if the audacious attorneys entertained any such hope they were speedily undeceived. Indeed, they had no sooner filed their application than the indignant jurist met their defiance by significantly offering them an opportunity to withdraw it, and upon their re-

[1] Frederick Philipse.

fusal he made short work of them and their attack.

"You thought to have gained a great deal of applause and popularity by opposing this Court as you did the Court of Exchequer," he exclaimed to the presumptuous counsel, "but you have brought it to this point that either we must go from the bench or you from the bar!" Whereupon he struck their names from the roll of practising attorneys and the prisoner was thus left unrepresented at the very outset of his fight. This sensational development, however, merely served to intensify the popular feeling, for John Chambers, another attorney, almost immediately undertook the defence, and at the last moment Andrew Hamilton, of Philadelphia, the most distinguished advocate of his day, volunteered his services in behalf of the accused.

Such was the situation on August 4, 1735, when the greatest crowd which Wall Street had ever harbored gathered at the City Hall clamoring for admission, and before it dispersed a long step had been taken toward American independence.

The little court-room to which only a small

percentage of the crowd gained admittance, presented a brilliant picture when the prisoner was called to the dock, for the judges wore the rich robes and long judicial wigs familiar to English courts, the lawyers were arrayed in the picturesque wigs and gowns officially prescribed for barristers, and all the functions and ceremonies of English legal procedure were carefully observed.[1] Moreover, the audience included almost all the prominent government officials appropriately attired for an affair of state, and many army officers whose smart uniforms contrasted sharply with the sombre but effective dress of the popular party. Never before had Wall Street witnessed a similar gathering, and it was never to see its like again, for a new era was dawning when the people opposed their rulers in that crowded court of law.

Hamilton opened the proceedings by admitting his client's publication of the papers in question,

[1] This is probably the first case in New York ever tried before a "struck" jury. Court order authorizing this was entered July 29, 1735.

Judge Smith states in his *History of New York* (vol. i., p. 316) that the New York judges and lawyers never wore gowns in colonial days, but there is evidence to the contrary at the date of Zenger's trial.

and announcing that he would rest his defence on the truth of the statements they contained. Thereupon an extraordinary legal battle ensued, the Attorney-General and the Chief-Justice joining in an attack upon the eminent Pennsylvanian, and endeavoring to ride rough-shod over his contentions. But Hamilton, though enfeebled by old age and ill-health, more than held his own, and when he at last acquired the right to address the jury, he rose to the occasion with the most powerful plea for freedom of the press that the New World had ever heard. So masterful, indeed, was his argument that the Chief-Justice felt constrained to counteract its influence by virtually directing the jury to convict. Nevertheless, the twelve good men, and true,[1] promptly returned a verdict of acquittal, and the moment the foreman announced this result the audience leaped to its feet and burst into a storm of cheering which De Lancey was powerless to suppress. Again and again he attempted to restore order, but one of the popular leaders practically defied

[1] Several well-known New York families were evidently represented on this jury, which included such names as Rutgers, Holmes, Man, Bell, Keteltas, Hildreth, and Goelet.

his authority, and with renewed cheers the exultant victors poured into Wall Street, where a roaring crowd instantly surrounded Hamilton and attempted to carry him off in triumph on its shoulders. That night the whole city was ablaze with enthusiasm, a grand banquet was given in Hamilton's honor, and all the popular leaders were cheered to the echo. Indeed, the public rejoicing continued throughout the following day, and when the successful advocate started for Philadelphia an enormous throng accompanied him to his barge, and his departure was honored by a salute of cannon. Nor was this the end, for some weeks later the Common Council awarded him the Freedom of the City in recognition of his disinterested services to the people, and the address conferring this distinction was conveyed to him [1] in a gold box ornamented with the arms of the city. Thus ended an event which has been called "the dawn of American liberty," and many of the scenes which Wall Street witnessed in later years can be clearly traced to the influence of this *cause célèbre*.

Indeed, from 1734 to 1770 the history of the

[1] By Alderman Stephen Bayard.

CITY HALL, WALL STREET, AUGUST 4, 1735
(See the descriptive note in the List of Illustrations.)

city is a record of constant collisions between the popular party and the royal Executive, and he was a strong man, indeed, who more than held his own. Governor Clarke proved unequal to the task, Clinton fought fiercely for ten years and then retired exhausted, Osborne killed himself on the eve of conflict, Sir Charles Hardy virtually surrendered all authority into the hands of Lieutenant-Governor De Lancey, Major-General Monckton practically abdicated in favor of Cadwallader Colden, and Sir Henry Moore was far from being the ruling power. Thus, in thirty-six years, the representative of the King was transformed from an autocrat into a figure-head, and further changes were already in prospect.

X

THE STAMP-ACT CONGRESS

MEANWHILE Wall Street, which had acclaimed the gorgeous inaugural processions of the incoming governors and speeded most of the retiring officials with jeers, had been altering its appearance for the better by abolishing the old slave market, which vanished in 1762, and in the same year street lamps were introduced. These public betterments were soon followed by the complete renovation of the City Hall and the removal of the whipping-post, pillory, stocks, and cage, and with its house thus put in order, Wall Street welcomed the first and perhaps the most notable popular assemblage recorded in the history of the United States.

It was with no blare of trumpets or any official ceremonies that this distinguished company convened in the City Hall on October 7, 1765; but on that day and in that building the American Revolution may fairly be said to have started, for the Stamp-Act Congress was the first representative body organized for the common protection of all the colonies against the mother-country, and in it the Continental Congress was plainly foreshadowed. No fewer than nine colonies were represented, and among the delegates who journeyed to Wall Street were Robert and Philip Livingston, James Otis, William Samuel Johnson, John Rutledge, Thomas McKean, and others,[1] whose names were to become household words and whose deeds were to enroll them among the founders of the nation. These men of unsuspected powers conducted their proceedings behind closed doors, but during their deliberations, which lasted three weeks, the interest of the whole country was centred on the narrow highway, and the address to the King and the memorials to the Houses of Parliament—the first of those remarkable state papers which won the admiration of Europe—were composed almost within shadow of Trinity Church.

[1] A full list of the delegates is to be found in the *New York Weekly Gazette and Mercury*, issue of October 14, 1765.

XI

THE PRELUDE TO THE REVOLUTION

THE Stamp-Act Congress was still in session when the first ship bearing the obnoxious stamps arrived in the harbor, and from that moment the calm deliberations of the visiting statesmen ceased to interest the excited city. Action and not argument now seemed imperative, and for several days turbulent crowds thronged the streets, and notices advocating violence were posted at every public meeting-place. Finally on the evening of November 1st the storm broke, and the residents of Wall Street, aroused by the sound of a tumult in the direction of the Fields,[1] rushed from their houses and then hastily retreated to bar their doors against the strangest mob which ever invaded a peaceful thoroughfare. Down Pearl (Queen) Street a torchlight procession was advancing with shouts and shots

[1] Now the City Hall Park.

and other alarming demonstrations, and at its head rumbled a gallows on wheels bearing an effigy of Lieutenant-Governor Colden, followed by another similar figure carried in a chair on the head of a stalwart negro. Hooting, jeering, and occasionally shooting at these effigies, several hundred sailors and rough, water-side characters bearing torches and lanterns swung into Wall Street, and on their heels followed a great throng of boisterous men. Suddenly, to the dismay of the householders anxiously watching the wild scene from behind their shuttered windows, the paraders halted before the house of one James McEvers, but their leaders immediately called for three cheers for this gentleman, who, through prudence or patriotism, had resigned his position as Stamp Distributor, and, the crowd, responding with an approving roar and a flourish of lanterns and torches, swept on toward the City Hall.[1] Brief as this delay was it had enabled the panic-stricken authorities to organize some slight resistance, and by the time the mob reached Broad Street its progress was

[1] *New York Weekly Gazette and Mercury*, and *The Weekly Post Boy*, November 7, 1765.

opposed by the Mayor, Aldermen,[1] and a squad of constables, who boldly attacked the bearers of the effigies and actually succeeded in tumbling their burdens into the street. Surprised by this vigorous assault, the rioters halted in confusion, but the moment they perceived that only a handful of men stood before them they pressed forward, carrying the officials off their feet, and in another moment they had gained the City Hall and were swarming up the narrow incline leading past the Presbyterian Church to Trinity. Here the leaders swung to the left, and with an exultant roar the mob followed, heading straight for Fort George, where the hated stamps had been deposited, and in a few minutes it was massed before the entrance clamoring for admission. No response being given to this angry demonstration, some of the more adventurous spirits broke into the Lieutenant-Governor's carriage-house, and, seizing one of the coaches, bundled the effigies into it and dragged it off in triumph, the others following with shouts of exultation.

[1] Among these bold officials were Nicholas Roosevelt and Cornelius Roosevelt, representing the West and the Out Wards of the city.

Again Wall Street was invaded, but this time the crowd assembled at the Merchants' Coffee-house, received the crude pageant with cheers as it passed on to the Fields, where a junction was formed with another mob and the whole force headed for the Battery. Once more a half-hearted attempt was made to gain admittance to the fort, but after hammering on the gate with their cudgels the ringleaders turned their attention to the coach-house, and, dragging out the Lieutenant-Governor's sleighs and carriages, heaped them together on Bowling Green, threw the effigies on top, and quickly turned the whole mass into a roaring bonfire, around which hundreds of men capered in a wild and sinister dance.

Thus ended this night of terror, but for the next two days the city remained in comparative quiet. Then anonymous placards and notices began to reappear, warning the authorities of further trouble if the stamps were not surrendered, and hasty conferences were held between the Mayor, the acting Governor and the leading citizens to concert measures for maintaining order. At first Colden was for meeting force with force; but finding little support for this policy, he finally compromised by sanctioning a semi-official promise that no use should be made of the stamps until further orders from England. But the "Sons of Liberty," who had undoubtedly organized the hostile demonstrations, were in no mood to accept such empty concessions and the only response to the Governor's proclamation was a notice calling another meeting in the Fields for the night of November 5th.

At this juncture the City Magistrates hurriedly convened in the City Hall, and an enormous throng gathered outside the building to learn the result of their deliberations. Finally a committee was appointed to urge that the stamps be surrendered into the custody of the local authorities, and the moment the men intrusted with this mission appeared on the street the crowd closed in and escorted them to the threshold of Fort George, where they halted in a silent but menacing mass. Very little would have sufficed at that critical moment to precipitate a violent conflict. Behind the feeble ramparts were gathered a few hundred armed but not over-reliable troops, and facing them an overwhelming army of determined and not too orderly citizens. Had either side provoked the other, or even had the parley between the Executive and the committee been unduly prolonged, the first bloodshed in the cause of independence would undoubtedly have occurred near Bowling Green. It was not long, however, before the committee reappeared and announced, amid a scene of wild rejoicing, that the acting Governor had yielded and would surrender the stamps to the Mayor. Welcome as this news was the crowd did not disperse, but hung about the Fort waiting the fulfilment of the official promise, and before long the gates opened and a strong guard marched out escorting the hated documents.

Then followed a triumphant return to Wall Street, the victorious populace surrounding the bearers of the captured papers, and accompanying them to the very steps of the City Hall, where the Mayor receipted for them, their surrender being the signal for an outburst which recalled the demonstrations accorded Hamilton's first victory for the people on the same spot thirty years before.

Some four months later the Stamp Act was repealed, largely through the efforts of William Pitt, in whose honor a marble statue was erected in Wall Street, which was rapidly becoming the centre of fashion and was soon to be the scene of many memorable events in the founding of the nation.

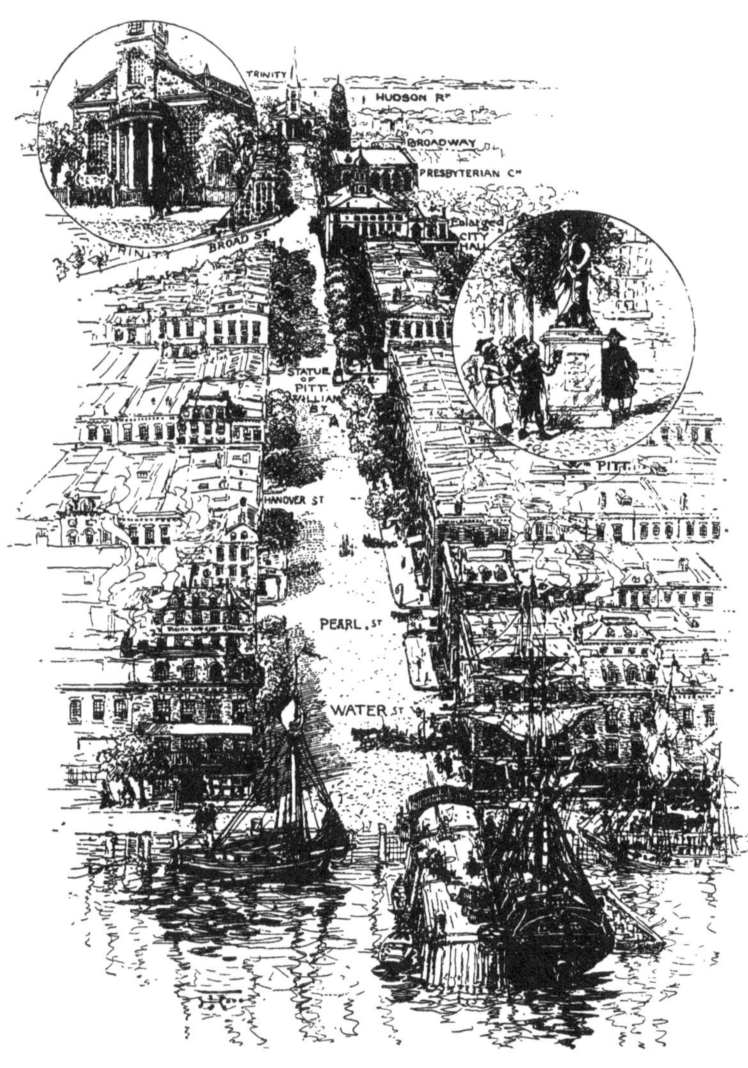

BIRD'S-EYE VIEW OF WALL STREET ABOUT 1774

XII

PAUL REVERE AND COMING EVENTS

A TRAVEL-STAINED horseman journeying down Broadway on Tuesday, May 17, 1774, turned his jaded mount to the left on reaching Trinity Church and passed into Wall Street unrecognized and scarcely noticed. The man was evidently a stranger, but cosmopolitan New York, with a population of nearly twenty-five thousand, was accustomed to the presence of visitor's, and there was nothing in the appearance of this one to attract attention beyond the fact that his clothes, saddle-bags, and horse were encrusted with mud, and that his tired animal suggested a long trip over difficult country. The rider himself, scarcely less exhausted than his horse, was a sturdily built fellow about forty years of age, with a clean-shaven, rather commonplace face, and the undistinguished bearing of a farmer or petty merchant. Certainly no one would have supposed him to be a man of artistic temperament or heroic mould, and yet he was an artist of no mean caliber, and his crudest sketches were destined to be cherished by future generations of hero-worshippers, for within a year he was to win undying fame and provide a stirring theme for song and story. Wall Street, however, saw no shadow of the coming event, and Paul Revere, illustrator and engraver, dentist, merchant, goldsmith, soldier, and "Constitutional Post-rider," passed quietly on his way, staring curiously at the busy scene unfolded to his gaze.

There must have been much that was strange and diverting to the provincial in the passing throngs—the venders of tea-water from the pump near the Collect pond, with their crude hogsheads carried in carts or set on wheels, the clumsy travelling coaches, the sedan-chairs, the gorgeously uniformed officers and officials, the groups of sombrely attired merchants—all the life and movement of the bustling commercial and official centre must have afforded a novel contrast to quiet Boston, with her port practically closed and her commerce almost dead. Yet, unfamiliar as his surroundings were, this was not Revere's first

WALL STREET IN 1774
(See the descriptive note in the List of Illustrations.)

visit to New York. Less than six months before he had carried the news of the Boston Tea-party to the local Sons of Liberty, but their headquarters were then near the Fields,[1] and this was possibly his first view of the street which was now almost without a rival in the fashionable quarter of the town.

Before him stretched a neat and attractive thoroughfare lined with stately shade-trees and handsome houses, whose dignified appearance demonstrated that their owners were men of substance, if not of fashion. At his left the Presbyterian Church still maintained its commanding position, and just beyond it lay the reconstructed City Hall, its upper stories, supported by arches, forming an arcade through which the pedestrians passed; but the hideous sugar refinery which had disfigured the neighborhood for many years had at last disappeared, and the Verplanck mansion and other handsome private dwellings now occupied its site. Beyond these on the same side of the street lay the McEvers mansion, before which the Stamp-tax rioters had paused in their wild march some nine years earlier, and in front

[1] Present City Hall Park.

of which now stood Pitt's marble statue, the work of Wilton, a famous sculptor, while in its immediate vicinity ranged the comfortable residences of the Thurmans, Banckers, Ludlows, Startins, Winthrops, Whites, Jaunceys, and other citizens of credit and more or less renown.

Riding by these attractive, home-like houses, Revere must have passed that of his friend and correspondent John Lamb,[1] one of the most active members in the Sons of Liberty, whose ceaseless agitation of popular rights had for some years been forcing the hands alike of friends and foes. Indeed, if any one individual could have been held accountable for the exciting scenes which Wall Street had recently experienced, the responsibility would probably have been laid at Lamb's well-appointed door. In fact, on the very day when Revere and his fellow-masqueraders were destroying the cargoes of the East India Company in Boston Harbor, John Lamb was rousing the merchants of New York to similar violence in the City Hall; and had a tea ship ar-

[1] Griswold, in his *American Court*, claims that Whigs like Lamb obtained no foothold in Wall Street till after the Revolution, but there is evidence that Lamb was an exception to this rule.

rived in the port at that juncture there is no doubt that his Wall Street audience would have quickly organized a Tea-party without paint or feathers. Fortunately or unfortunately, however, no vessel had appeared at that crisis; but about four months later, when the *London* sailed into the harbor, a Vigilance Committee promptly boarded her without the least effort at disguise and bundled her objectionable merchandise into the sea. This had occurred on Friday, April 22, 1774, and the very next day Wall Street witnessed an exhibition of the popular temper as unique as it was significant.

About the same time that the *London* came to anchor in the lower bay another vessel known as the *Nancy* arrived with a cargo of tea, imported expressly for the purpose of testing the strength of the non-importation agreement. Her commander, Captain Lockyer, made no secret of his mission, and the Vigilance Committee finally permitted him to visit the city for the purpose of consulting his consignees; but when those gentlemen prudently refused to receive his cargo the worthy captain was ordered to sail for England at the earliest possible moment.

Meanwhile notices had been posted throughout the city, summoning all friends of the country to assemble on Murray's Wharf, at the foot of Wall Street, on the day of Lockyer's departure, and give him a send-off which he would be likely to remember and report to his friends across the sea. Accordingly, at eight o'clock on Saturday morning, April 23d, bells began ringing all over the city, more and more joining in the chorus, until every clapper in town was swinging save those of the loyal City Hall and King's College, and at this prearranged signal all sorts and conditions of men began streaming toward the rendezvous, some of them accompanied by brass-bands, and all the shipping on the river-front displayed its brightest bunting. For an hour the crowds continued to pour into Wall Street, massing in front of the Merchants' Coffee-house, on the southeast corner of Wall and Water streets, where the offending mariner had taken up his abode, and the moment he showed himself on the balcony in the custody of a committee of citizens a deafening roar of cheers and a bedlam of bells greeted his appearance. No disorder of any sort was attempted, however, and when quiet

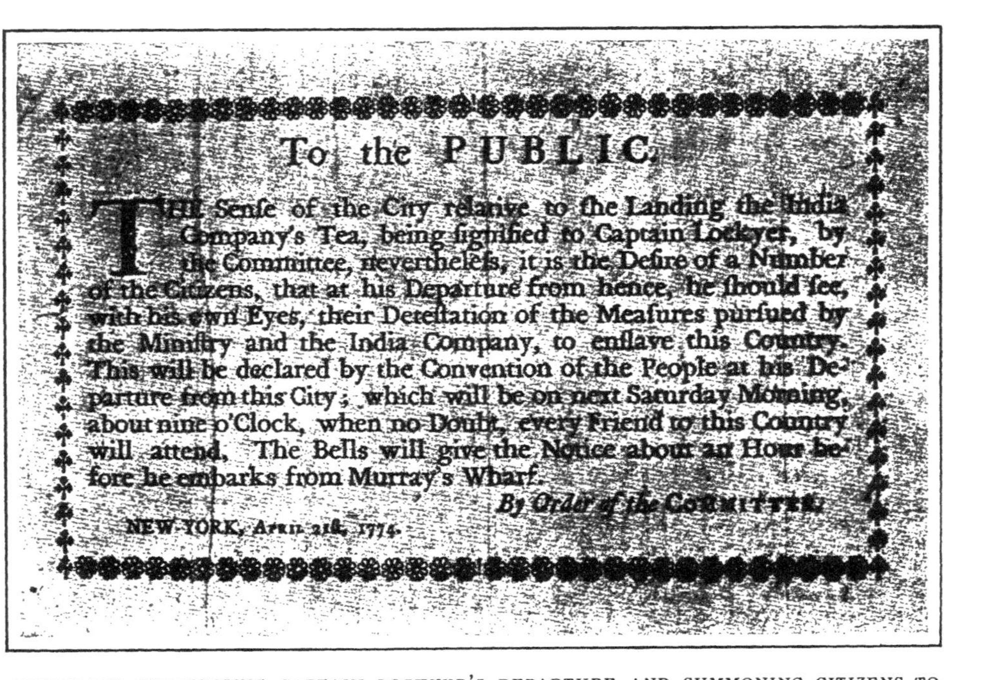

To the PUBLIC.

THE Sense of the City relative to the Landing the India Company's Tea, being signified to Captain Lockyer, by the Committee, nevertheless, it is the Desire of a Number of the Citizens, that at his Departure from hence, he should see, with his own Eyes, their Detestation of the Measures pursued by the Ministry and the India Company, to enslave this Country. This will be declared by the Convention of the People at his Departure from this City; which will be on next Saturday Morning, about nine o'Clock, when no Doubt, every Friend to this Country will attend. The Bells will give the Notice about an Hour before he embarks from Murray's Wharf.

By Order of the COMMITTEE.

NEW-YORK, April 21st, 1774.

BROADSIDE ANNOUNCING CAPTAIN LOCKYER'S DEPARTURE AND SUMMONING CITIZENS TO MURRAY'S WHARF ON WALL STREET

(See the descriptive note in the List of Illustrations)

was restored the committee solemnly introduced their victim to the crowd and signalled the bands, which burst into "God Save the King." During this demonstration of loyalty the captain was escorted with great ceremony into the street, where a lane was forced for him through the cheering multitude to the wharf, from which he boarded a pilot-boat, accompanied by a deputation charged with the duty of seeing him safely off Sandy Hook, and amid the booming of cannon and other wild demonstrations of rejoicing he sailed away to carry the news of his significant reception to ears that would not hear.

XIII

THE MERCHANTS' COFFEE-HOUSE

THESE events must have been known to Paul Revere, and possibly they were in his mind as he jogged through Wall Street,[1] for he was the accredited messenger not only of the Sons of Liberty, but also of the Committee of Correspondence, and it was at their unofficial headquarters, the Merchants' Coffee-house, that he undoubtedly alighted.

Of all the historic buildings which figure in Wall Street's story, this unpretentious tavern is fairly entitled to a place apart. Erected about 1740,[2] on what was then practically the water's

[1] The exact route followed by Revere cannot now be positively identified. He left Boston May 14, 1774; was almost three days on the road; entered the city by the Bowery, or Boston Post Road, and his despatch was for the Committee of Correspondence, some of whose members were usually to be found at the Merchants' Coffee-house.

[2] The first reference to this historic building appears to be in the *Weekly Post-Boy*, January 16, 1744 (No. 52, p.

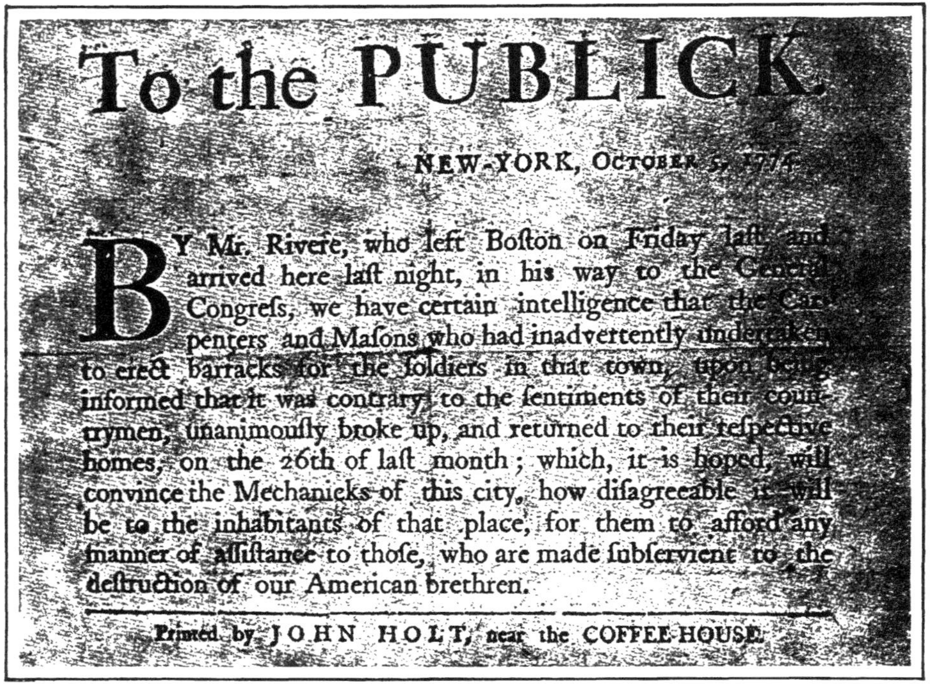

To the PUBLICK.

NEW-YORK, OCTOBER 5, 1774.

BY Mr. Rivere, who left Boston on Friday last, and arrived here last night, in his way to the General Congress, we have certain intelligence that the Carpenters and Masons who had inadvertently undertaken to erect barracks for the soldiers in that town, upon being informed that it was contrary to the sentiments of their countrymen, unanimously broke up, and returned to their respective homes, on the 26th of last month; which, it is hoped, will convince the Mechanicks of this city, how disagreeable it will be to the inhabitants of that place, for them to afford any manner of assistance to those, who are made subservient to the destruction of our American brethren.

Printed by JOHN HOLT, near the COFFEE-HOUSE.

BROADSIDE ANNOUNCING AN ARRIVAL OF PAUL REVERE'S IN NEW YORK
(See the descriptive note in the List of Illustrations.)

edge, at a time when privateersmen and other adventurous sons of the sea frequented the port to compare notes and transact business of a kind best consummated over a glass of grog, behind walls devoid of ears, it had immediately become a sort of maritime exchange whose secrets never leaked and whose rear doors were exceedingly convenient for customers who preferred to be within hail of their small boats. With the passing of the privateersmen and other less admirable water-side characters, however, it gradually developed from a sailors' snug harbor into a place of general resort whose patrons were so fastidious that the adjoining slave market had to be removed for their benefit,[1] and from that time onward its popularity steadily increased, until its guests included all the best people in the community and its influence was that of a civic forum.

4), where it is mentioned in an advertisement dated November, 1743.

[1] "Said Meal (Slave) Markett greatly Obstructs the agreeable prospect of the East River which those that live in Wall St. would Otherwise enjoy; that it Occasions a Dirty Street Offensive to the Inhabitants on each side and Disagreeable to those that pass and Repass to and from the Coffee House a place of Great Resort."—*Minutes of Common Council*, vol. vi., p. 283. New York City Hall.

There was nothing imposing either in the exterior or the interior of this celebrated inn. All that is known of its outward appearance is that it was a three-storied structure, with a large room on the first floor, another on the second, a piazza or balcony on the front, and a platform or porch on the side, and its interior appointments were in keeping with this very modest architectural plan. The two "long rooms," however, witnessed many a famous meeting and consultation, and their part in the prelude to the Revolution was of the first importance. Here it was that the demonstrations against the military occupation and rule of Boston had taken place in 1769; here some of the most interesting conferences of the Friends of Liberty and Trade were held; here Isaac Sears and other radicals urged the seizure of the stamps; here Lockyer was accorded his mock reception; here began the demonstration against the closing of the port of Boston, which ended in the burning of Lord North in effigy before a crowded balcony; here all the political leaders foregathered; and here, on May 17, 1774, Paul Revere arrived with his despatch to the Committee of Correspond-

WALL STREET FROM WATER STREET TO THE EAST RIVER
(See the descriptive note in the List of Illustrations.)

ence, just reorganized into the Committee of Fifty.

On its face the message which Revere delivered at this famous tavern was not of extraordinary interest, for it merely reported the resolutions adopted at Faneuil Hall, requesting New York's co-operation in suspending trade with England until the ministry should reopen the port of Boston; but the reply to this communication was epoch-making, for it undoubtedly gave the first impulse to the founding of a national government.

Before the famous post-rider was fairly on the road again, headed for Philadelphia,[1] a meeting of merchants and other citizens was called at the Coffee-house to nominate a committee to respond to the proposals contained in his despatch, and the existing Committee of Fifty was reappointed with one addi ional member. Of the assemblage gathered on this occasion Gouverneur Morris wrote: "I stood on the balcony [of the Coffee-house], and on my right hand were ranged all the people of property, with some poor dependents, and on the other all the tradesmen, etc.,

[1] May 19, 1774.

who thought it worth their while to leave their daily labor for the good of the country." It is characteristic of the man that Morris, then in his twenty-third year, should have made himself the centre of this eventful scene, but he was undoubtedly a leader, for in New York, as in other States, the Revolution was the work of youth tempered by almost precocious maturity of judgment. Among those who, with Morris, were moulding history in Wall Street at this critical period were John Jay, aged twenty-eight; Alexander Hamilton, seventeen; Robert Livingston, twenty-seven; Marinus Willett, thirty-three; Alexander McDougall, forty-three; Isaac Low, thirty-nine; and Isaac Sears, the fire-eating veteran, forty-five. Some of these men were on the committee intrusted with the duty of answering the Massachusetts proposals, and it is doubtful if any other body of citizens ever afforded as rare a combination of youth and intellectual maturity. There were, of course, a few hot-heads among them, and Alexander McDougall, disgusted with his associates' conservatism, angrily withdrew and attempted to force their hands. In this he was not successful, but the response which was finally adopted by the majority on May 23, 1774, was certainly not the utterance of timorous senility. Indeed, it was nothing less than the first proposal for a convention of delegates from all the colonies, and when Paul Revere received it on his return from Philadelphia, Wall Street had won historic honors; for of this paper formulated in her famous Coffee-house came the Continental Congress.

XIV

THE REVOLUTION AT WALL STREET'S DOORS

LESS than one year[1] later Israel Bessel, another post-rider, came spurring into the Bowery Road from Boston, breaking the quiet of a Sabbath morning by roaring startling news at every passing group of citizens; and as the congregations of Trinity and the Presbyterian church issued from their noonday services he burst upon them with tidings that the battle of Lexington had been fought and won four days before. In an instant he was surrounded by an anxious throng eagerly clamoring for details, and Wall Street was soon in a state of wild commotion, loyalists and patriots scattering to protect their families and property, each man suspecting and fearing the other, and all almost equally dismayed by the news. The patriots were the first to recover from the shock, however, and, headed by

[1] April 23, 1775.

WALL STREET, SUNDAY, APRIL 23, 1775
(See the descriptive note in the List of Illustrations.)

Isaac Sears and some of the boldest Sons of Liberty, a band of citizens hastily assembled, and, taking possession of the City Hall, seized five hundred stand of arms deposited there for the troops, demanded and received the keys of the Custom-house, closed the building, and virtually deposed the royal government.

From that moment all business was suspended in the city, and between April 24 and May 1, 1775, confusion reigned supreme. Then the ablest men in the community assumed control, and calling a mass-meeting at the Merchants' Coffee-house, which had practically become the seat of government, organized a provisional Committee of One Hundred to administer the public business. By the orders of this committee the city was virtually placed under martial law, the shops and factories were closed, the streets were patrolled by improvised bands of militia, all available arms and ammunition were seized, crude preparations were made for resisting an attack, and many timorous loyalists abandoned their houses and sought safety at their country-seats. Meanwhile some of the King's troops had been allowed to enter the city, the loyalist members of the committee feeling that their presence would insure order, but when they made an attempt to appropriate the spare arms deposited in their barracks, Marinus Willett forced an armed guard to surrender this booty, and the carts containing the weapons were triumphantly escorted by a great throng of citizens up Broadway, past the head of Wall Street, to Abraham Van Dyck's ball alley at John Street, where they were placed under lock and key.

Up to this time the leading patriots and loyalists of the city had worked together for the maintenance of order, but anything more than a temporary truce was impossible, and before long the Committee of One Hundred was split into warring factions and party feeling began to run high. Numerically the patriots were in a vast majority, but many men of property and influence were loud in their expressions of loyalty and bitter in their denunciations of the provisional government, whose legality they stoutly denied. Under such circumstances more or less disorder was inevitable, and residence in the city was made extremely uncomfortable for many of the outspoken loyalists. Indeed, some of the more obnoxious were stripped to the skin and ridden on rails through Wall Street, greatly to the scandal of the highly respectable denizens of that most decorous neighborhood.

Such was the condition of affairs in April, 1776, when Washington arrived to oppose the British forces dislodged from Boston, and under his energetic leadership the active preparations for defence which had already been begun were pushed, until the whole appearance of the town was practically transformed. Fortifications were hastily erected on the water-front; batteries were planted at various posts of vantage; breastworks and barricades were thrown across the streets; bullets were cast out of lead taken from the roofs of the houses; and some of the buildings were loop-holed for street fighting and a house-to-house resistance. Of these crude defences Wall Street boasted a battery masked in the cellar of a house on the East River, a breastwork near the Coffee-house, and McDougall's battery, stationed a little to the west of Trinity, which continued to conduct its services as though nothing whatever had happened. Indeed, the clergy and congregation of that church did not seem to realize that the Revolution was a fact even when Washington arrived upon the scene, but within a few weeks the war was brought home to them in most extraordinary fashion.

The Reverend Charles Inglis was then assistant rector of the parish, and Washington had not been long in the city before an officious member of his staff called upon the clergyman and requested him to omit the customary prayers for the King, which had been loyally read at all services without the least regard for the existing political conditions. But Mr. Inglis, though a non-combatant, was evidently a believer in the Church militant and a most ardent supporter of the crown, for he promptly refused the request, which Washington disavowed as soon as it was brought to his attention. Certainly the King never so needed the prayers of his faithful subjects as he did at that moment, when peace negotiations were impending, but this was not the popular view. Nevertheless, the services were conducted for some weeks without alteration or interruption, while the contending forces prepared for what promised to be the bitterest struggle of the war.

One Sunday morning in May, however, a motley crew of about one hundred and fifty armed men, preceded by a fife and drum corps, invaded Wall Street and headed straight for Trinity. Whether they were soldiers or not is uncertain, but they carried bayonets on their guns and were apparently under some sort of military control. Marching to the brisk tap of drums, they passed through the street, crossed Broadway, entered the church, and swept up the aisle, drums beating and fifes shrilling in deafening uproar. Appalled by this desecrating intrusion, the congregation sat aghast, not knowing what to expect; but the white-robed clergyman calmly stood his ground, confronted the invaders, and outfaced them. Indeed, the moment the drums and fifes ceased he proceeded with the services as though nothing had happened, and conducting it with admirable dignity to the very end without the omission of a single word, drove the armed rabble into ignominious retreat.

This was the last, or one of the last, services ever held in the church, however, for its authorities soon thought best to close its doors, and within four months it was totally destroyed by fire. Meanwhile Wall Street listened to the Declaration of Independence, which was read from the steps of the City Hall on July 16, 1776, to a small band of patriots whose enthusiasm prompted them to invade the court-room and tear down the royal coat of arms, which they then proceeded to burn on the spot where Zenger's *Journal* had been consigned to the flames, thus affording a precedent for wanton destruction that was to cost the city dear before many months had passed. In fact, when the British troops entered the town two months later they looted the City Hall library without mercy, bartering the valuable books for drink, and completely scattering what would now be a unique collection. The statue of Pitt was also wrecked almost beyond recognition, but there were few who regretted its fate, for Pitt had alienated many Americans by his apparent hostility to their independence, and the statue had already been somewhat defaced before the loyalists completed the work of destruction.

With these acts of vandalism Wall Street began a long and bitter experience. Indeed, before the British troops had fairly established themselves in New York the great fire of September 21, 1776, which obliterated a large part of the city, laid Trinity in ruins, and this disaster, wrongly attributed to rebel sympathizers, resulted in such harsh measures against the American residents that many of them fled, abandoning their houses to the enemy.

XV

OCCUPATION AND EVACUATION

IT did not take long for the army of occupation to appropriate all the available property in the street to its own purposes. The City Hall was immediately transformed into a guard-house and prison, and fortunate indeed were those who were incarcerated there, for they received humane treatment and escaped the horrors which were daily enacted in the sugar-houses and hulks where the majority of American prisoners were confined. One of the earliest inmates of this Wall Street prison was General Charles Lee, and it would have been well for him had he been detained there until the end of the war. He was, however, soon set at liberty, and his subsequent conduct not only led to his disgrace, but came perilously close to wrecking the American cause.

Another famous Wall Street building was likewise utilized for the purposes of the army, for the Presbyterian Church was pressed into service as a hospital for the British sick and wounded, and to adapt it to this use it was practically dismantled. These changes, however, merely marked the beginning of the end, for every house vacated by the Americans was immediately placed at the disposal of a British general or official; and so great was the demand for residential property for the housing of these gentlemen that the dwellings of all rebels were marked with a broad R to subject them to confiscation.

Wall Street thus practically became the headquarters of the army of occupation, and the entire neighborhood assumed a military air. General Knyphausen, the German commander of the Hessians, took possession of the McEvers mansion; General Robertson, the Royal Governor, established himself in the Verplanck mansion, between William and Nassau streets,[1] and this same dwelling also sheltered Benedict Arnold for a short time after he turned traitor. General Riedesel, the Hessian, was another commander who resided in the once fashionable highway, and the famous Coffee-house quickly became the

[1] Almost on the site of the present Assay Office.

favorite resort of all the army and navy officers quartered in the town.

Under these conditions the whole aspect of the street gradually changed, its buildings steadily deteriorated, and before long very little remained of its former glory. In the summer of 1779 a feeble attempt was made to turn the grounds surrounding the blackened ruins of Trinity into a place of fashionable promenade, and with this idea they were enclosed with wooden railings painted green, lamps were hung in the trees, under which benches were placed, and concerts were given by the garrison bands, to which only people of quality were admitted. This was the only effort, however, which was made to restore Wall Street's prestige, and the following winter destroyed its last claim to beauty; for during the unprecedentedly cold weather which permitted the transport of cannon to Staten Island over the ice-covered bay, almost all its stately shade-trees were sacrificed to provide fuel for the families of Generals Knyphausen, Riedesel, and other officers. From this time onward desolation and decay marked the highway for their own, and as the war drew to a close its condition passed from bad to worse; for the British naturally took no pains to preserve property which they were soon to restore to its former owners, and dirt and débris were allowed to accumulate, until every street was a rubbish-heap lined with wrecked, dismantled, or dilapidated buildings.

Such was the condition of Wall Street on November 25, 1783, when Brigadier-General Henry Jackson, in command of about eight hundred men, stationed at McGowan's Pass, set his troops in motion for the Collect, or Fresh Water Pond, on the outskirts of the town, where he halted about noon under the orders of General Henry Knox, deputed by Washington to take possession of New York. At the same hour the rear guard of the British army of 6500 was marching down Broadway to embark for Staten Island, their brilliant uniforms and perfect equipment affording a brave sight for all beholders, and a little later in the afternoon one of Sir Guy Carleton's staff reported to the American commander that the last of his troops were on the transports at the Battery. This was the word which General Knox had been eagerly awaiting, and within a few minutes of its receipt the American column, composed of detachments of Massachusetts infantry, New York artillery, a militia company, and a troop of horse under Captain Stakes, was swinging toward the heart of the city. Down the Bowery road they swept with the stride of seasoned veterans, their motley uniforms incrusted with mud and showing signs of rough campaigning, their tarnished arms and torn colors presenting a sharp contrast to the display of the evacuating host. There was every evidence of discipline and training, however, in the movements and carriage of these weather-beaten soldiers, and as they passed through Chatham Square to Pearl (Queen) Street great crowds of enthusiastic citizens welcomed them with cheers, and falling in on either side of the conquering column, accompanied its march.

Then came the great moment for which Wall Street had waited and suffered for over seven years, and up the devastated highway, thronged with a joyous multitude, swung the tattered but stalwart ranks to the business-like tap of drums and the music of exultant cheers. Onward they swept, past the headless statue of Pitt; past shabby dwellings, which their exiled owners would

New-York, Nov. 24, 178[illegible]

The Committee appointed to conduct the Order of receiving their Excellencies Governor CLINTON and General WASHINGTON,

BEG Leave to inform their Fellow-Citizens, that the Troops, under the Command of Major-General KNOX, will take Possession of the City at the Hour agreed on, Tuesday next; as soon as this may be performed, he will request the Citizens who may be assembled on Horseback, at the Bowling-Green, the lower End of the Broad-Way, to accompany him to meet their Excellencies Governor CLINTON and General WASHINGTON, at the Bull's Head, in the Bowery---the Citizens on Foot to assemble at or near the Tea-water-Pump at Fresh-water.

ORDER of PROCESSION.

A Party of Horse will precede their Excellencies and be on their flanks---after the General and Governor, will follow the Lieutenant-Governor and Members of the Council for the temporary Government of the Southern Parts of the State---The Gentlemen on Horse-back, eight in Front---those on Foot, in the Rear of the Horse, in like Manner. Their Excellencies, after passing down Queen-Street, and the Line of Troops up the Broadway, will a-light at CAPE's Tavern.

The Committee hope to see their Fellow-Citizens, conduct themselves with Decency and Decorum on this joyful Occasion.

CITIZENS TAKE CARE!!!

THE Inhabitants are hereby informed, that Permission has been obtained from the Commandant, to form themselves in patroles this night, and that every order requisite will be given to the guards, as well to aid and assist, as to give protection to the patroles: And that the countersign will be given to THOMAS TUCKER, No. [illegible], Water-Street, from whom it can be obtained, if necessary.

BROADSIDE ANNOUNCING WASHINGTON'S ENTRY INTO NEW YORK

(See the descriptive note in the List of Illustrations.)

scarcely have recognized; past the head of Broad Street, where the whipping-post had stood; past the dilapidated City Hall, where the Stamp Act Congress had assembled; up the slight incline, down which many a royal governor had paraded and along which countless throngs jostle and hurry to-day; past the dismantled Presbyterian Church, where Whitefield and Jonathan Edwards had preached, to the mournful ruins of Trinity. Then, wheeling to the right, these representatives of the victorious armies lined up in Broadway near Cape's Tavern,[1] bravely displaying the arms of New York State upon its sign, and on that historic spot, where Etienne De Lancey had built his home, they halted and stood at parade-rest till a salute of thirteen guns announced that the American flag floated over Fort George and that the Revolution was ended.

On the evening of that day of days Washington attended a banquet in Wall Street. Its golden age was dawning.

[1] About 115 Broadway.

XVI

WALL STREET THE CENTRE OF GOVERNMENT

WITH the last exultant echo of Evacuation Day Wall Street relapsed into the lethargy which had long pervaded the entire community. Many American cities had endured grievous hardships during the war; a few had been pillaged and partially burned; more than one had been practically obliterated; but for seven years New York had been remorselessly exploited to the point of exhaustion. Indeed, the city which the British abandoned in the fall of 1783 bore very little resemblance to the social and commercial centre they had wrested from Washington in the first year of the Revolution. Much of it was in an indescribable state of dilapidation and decay, part of it was in absolute ruins, and all of it was fairly reeking with dirt. In fact, the whole aspect of the place, with its empty houses and vacant streets patrolled by herds of prowling hogs, suggested a deserted village, and this is what it had virtually become. Of the twenty-five thousand inhabitants it had boasted in 1776 not more than twelve thousand remained at the end of the war, and those were by no means the flower of the population. Many of the best people had taken refuge in their country-houses at the very first sign of trouble; all the patriots of ability and character had retired with Washington's retreating forces; most of the influential loyalists had anticipated the withdrawal of the royal troops, and between these various emigrations New York had lost all its leading citizens, many of whom had gone never to return. Certainly the remaining residents did not display any extraordinary energy or public spirit after the army of occupation departed, and for some months the wasted city made no effort to revive its commerce or set its dismantled house in order.

By February, 1784, however, a number of familiar faces began to reappear, and early in that month a small group of forceful men gathered in John Simmons's Tavern, a little wooden building lying at the northwest corner of Wall and Nassau streets, to install James Duane as first

American Mayor of New York. In view of the impoverished condition of the community this public-spirited citizen had requested that the inauguration ceremonies should be conducted without expense or display; but why Simmons's Tavern should have been selected for such an occasion is not altogether certain. It is probable, however, that the City Hall, which had served for so many years as a prison, was not yet fit for civic duty, and that the inn was the nearest available meeting-place; but it may well be that the popularity of its proprietor deprived the Merchants' Coffee-house of adding this event to its long list of historic honors, for John Simmons was something of a local celebrity.[1] Indeed, the fat, good-natured countenance of this rotund boniface was for many years one of the familiar sights of Wall Street, over which he used to preside, squatting on his doorstep and exchanging salutations with all the passers-by, and the story that part of his tavern had to be torn down to remove his ponderous body when he died is a well-authenticated tradition of the times.

[1] Washington attended a banquet at Simmons's Tavern on the evening of Evacuation Day.

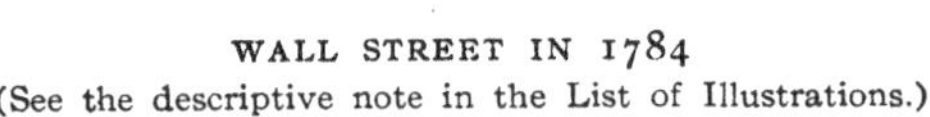

WALL STREET IN 1784
(See the descriptive note in the List of Illustrations.)

James Duane,[1] who was thus unceremoniously invested with the chief magistracy, was a man of wealth and refinement, whose long and efficient public service thoroughly qualified him for his task; and the other officials who were sworn in as his associates were energetic citizens whose achievements were already upon record. Marinus Willett, who became Sheriff, was the Revolutionary hero who had halted the British troops in Broad Street at the beginning of the war and prevented them from appropriating the arms of the local garrison. Richard Varick, who was appointed Recorder, had been one of Washington's junior secretaries, and had also served under General Schuyler; and Daniel Phœnix, who undertook the office of Chamberlain, was a merchant whose services as a member of the Sons of Liberty and the Committee of One Hundred entitled him to a high place in the public confidence. In fact, the task of establishing order out of chaos could scarcely have been placed in stronger hands, and the whole town assumed a

[1] Duane's country-seat was at Gramercy Park, so named from the Krom messie (or "Crooked little knife"), a stream running across it.

more cheerful air as soon as the new government entered upon the performance of its arduous duties.

Business was, of course, practically dead, but the Chamber of Commerce had been keeping up a flicker of life with its meetings at the Merchants' Coffee-house, and on April 13, 1784, it was duly incorporated by the New York Legislature, and immediately began systematic work for a revival of trade. There was one field of activity in the prostrate city, however, which needed no encouragement, and that was litigation. Throughout the whole State, but particularly in the cities, the ownership of property was in serious dispute, and what with the conflicting colonial and State laws and the various confiscations, restorations, seizures, and claims under cover of military authority, no one knew what his rights or liabilities were, and confusion reigned supreme. Moreover, in the face of these legal tangles and complications, all the Tory advocates had been disbarred, and for once at least in the history of New York the supply of lawyers did not equal the demand.

ALEXANDER HAMILTON
(See the descriptive note in the List of Illustrations.)

XVII

HAMILTON AND THE NEW YORK BAR

INTO this land of promise two newly fledged lawyers hurried in the winter of 1783, and among the first shingles displayed on Wall Street was that of Alexander Hamilton, while almost around the corner Aaron Burr began his brilliant and eventful professional career.[1] Had the latter been less resourceful and energetic, however, he would not have been numbered among the earliest arrivals, for the rules governing admission to the bar were strict, and he had served less than one of the required three years' legal apprenticeship. But no such obstacle could daunt a man of Burr's caliber, and he straightway journeyed to Albany and presented his case before the court in person. He could have completed his apprenticeship years ago, he argued, had he not

[1] Hamilton's office was at No. 58 (now 33) Wall Street; Burr's was at No. 10 Little Queen (Cedar) Street.

been employed in the service of the army, and no rule could be intended to injure one whose only misfortune was having sacrificed his time, his constitution, and his fortune to his country. This appeal naturally won the court, and the rules having been suspended, the candidate easily passed the required examination and hastened to New York, where he speedily acquired an enormous practice. Indeed, for a time Burr and Hamilton had few rivals in the field, but in July, 1784, John Jay [1] returned from a successful mission to Europe, and with his advent, which was marked by a public reception in Wall Street [2] and the presentation of the freedom of the city, a formidable competitor for legal honors was added to the rapidly growing list. But although the roll of the bar soon included over forty practising

[1] Jay's office was at No. 8 Broad Street.

[2] Other events associated with Wall Street in general and the City Hall in particular are the reception to Sir John Temple, the first Consul-General from Great Britain (November 24, 1784); the appointment of Thomas Jefferson as Minister to France (March 10, 1784); the Remonstrance to Great Britain against infractions of the Treaty of Peace requiring the removal of garrisons and the celebration in honor of the first successful voyage of a trading vessel from the United States to China and return (May, 1785).

attorneys, Hamilton and Burr virtually had the pick and choice of business, and the judgment displayed by each man in exercising his preference was exceedingly characteristic, for Burr never took a case unless he felt sure of winning it, and Hamilton would advocate any cause in which he thoroughly believed. In fact, he had not been long in practice before he risked his popularity and even imperilled his life by defending a rich Tory sued by a poor woman under the terms of the Trespass Act.[1] This law had been passed for the express purpose of penalizing loyalists, and no better opportunity for aiding a needy citizen at the expense of the common enemy had yet occurred. Under such circumstances the defence was not only a forlorn-hope, but a most ungrateful task. Yet Hamilton boldly attacked the law, declaring that it violated the provisions of the treaty of peace guaranteeing protection to the Tories in the enjoyment of their property rights, and so ably did he present his case that he carried the day in spite of popular clamor. The affair was not allowed to end there, however, for a newspaper war ensued in which the vic-

[1] This case was known as Rutgers *vs.* Waddington.

torious counsel used his pen with such effect that a group of his opponents conspired to challenge him successively until one of them should silence him in a duel, but the murderous plan was promptly exposed and abandoned. This notable legal triumph was achieved in the Mayor's Court, which was then held in a small building at the southwest corner of Wall and Broad streets, and here many of New York's most famous lawyers received their preliminary training. The men with whom Wall Street thus became acquainted, besides Burr, Jay, and Hamilton, were James Kent, Brockholst Livingston, Morgan Lewis, Robert Troup, Egbert Benson, Abraham De Peyster, Josiah Ogden Hoffman, and John Lawrence, some of whom were destined to become jurists of international fame. It was on the whole an extraordinarily youthful bar, for in 1784 Jay was only thirty-nine, Benson thirty-eight, Lewis thirty, Burr twenty-eight, Hamilton and Livingston twenty-seven, and Kent twenty-one; but some of these men had already given high proofs of their constructive talents, and they were soon engaged in re-establishing credit and promoting plans for civic betterment. Early in

OLD WATCH-HOUSE
(See the descriptive note in the List of Illustrations.)

1784 the Bank of New York was organized under Hamilton's guidance at the Merchants' Coffee-house,[1] and that same historic building had the honor of witnessing the first practical movement against slavery; for there, close to the site of the old slave market, were held the early meetings of the Society for the Manumission of Slaves, of which Jay subsequently became the president.

[1] The bank was first housed in the Walton Mansion, 156 Queen (Pearl) Street; later at 11 Hanover Square, and later still at No. 48 Wall Street.

XVIII

THE CONTINENTAL CONGRESS

MEANWHILE, Wall Street had been gradually clearing away its seven years' accumulation of dirt and wreckage, and by June, 1784, the Presbyterian Church, which had been practically dismantled in transforming it into an army hospital, was sufficiently repaired to welcome its returning congregation. No immediate effort was made, however, to rebuild Trinity, and for some years its melancholy ruins stared down a sadly dilapidated highway. Of course the houses which had once been its pride were still standing, but they had been roughly handled, and their owners could not afford to put them in proper condition; so the street remained shabby and neglected, and such was its condition when the Continental Congress announced its intention of making its headquarters in New York. Here was a great opportunity for the struggling city, for the presence of Congress, impotent as that body had become, would undoubtedly enhance its importance and prestige, but the civic authorities were ill-prepared to take advantage of the opportunity. Indeed, there were no suitable accommodations available for the visiting legislators, and the City Hall, which was finally placed at their disposal, was not much more than habitable. Nevertheless, the municipality offered the best it had, surrendering virtually the whole of the renovated City Hall and removing its own officials and records to the building on the southwest corner of Wall and Broad streets, which housed the Mayor's Court. Thus in 1785 all the representatives of the national as well as the municipal and State authority were concentrated in Wall Street,[1] and here daily congregated such men as John Hancock, Rufus King, Nathan Dane, Charles Pinckney, Richard Henry Lee, James Monroe, James Madison, and other distinguished statesmen of national repute, who with the lawyers and city officials in the

[1] Here, on July 13, 1787, was passed the famous Ordinance of 1787 which dedicated the great Northwest to freedom, and virtually determined the slavery struggle which was even then beginning.

building on the opposite corner constituted the Wall-Street men of their day.

The presence of the Continental Congress and the steady influx of visitors soon brought about a sharp demand for accommodations in the residence section of the city, and, while the price of almost everything else was falling, rents in Wall Street rose so that it was impossible to obtain even a very modest dwelling for less than £70 and taxes—an exorbitant figure in those days—and this naturally affected the price of land. Not many sales occurred, however, for in 1786[1] the street experienced what was probably its first financial panic, and such was the stringency of the money - market that cash practically disappeared from circulation. Indeed, credit throughout the whole country was almost suspended, and the conflicting laws of the various States discouraged business enterprise and threatened the complete extinction of trade.

Such was the situation when the great struggle

[1] According to a contemporary writer in the press, affairs in the city were generally deplorable for he bursts forth: "*Cash—O Cash! why hast thou deserted the standard of Liberty and made poverty and dissipation our distinguishing characteristics?*"

began for the formation of a permanent national government, and into this contest Hamilton plunged with the ardor of an enthusiast and all the unselfishness of a true patriot. There was much in the proposed Constitution which he did not approve, and his splendid legal practice could not be neglected without great personal sacrifice; but from the fall of 1786 to the summer of 1788 he worked unremittingly with voice and pen for the cause of the Union, and it was during this critical period that he wrote and published the famous "Federalist" papers which so profoundly affected the result. No less than sixty-three of those eighty-five brilliant essays were written by Hamilton in his office, No. 33 (then 58) Wall Street, and had the highway no other claim to historic interest its association with that epoch-making achievement would suffice to assure it national fame. Despite the stupendous efforts of the Federal leaders, however, and the strong support of almost the entire city, there seemed very little chance that the State of New York would ratify the Constitution, for the country districts were bitterly opposed to its adoption, and their representatives commanded a majority of the votes. Nevertheless, Hamilton continued to fight with unabated courage, and on July 26, 1788, he succeeded in turning the hostile majority into a minority by a narrow margin of three votes, and returned triumphant to the city, where great crowds gathered in Wall Street and welcomed him with cheers, while all the bells in town were rung and a salute of eleven guns was fired in his honor.

Four weeks after this momentous victory Wall Street was alive with workmen removing the blackened ruins of Trinity Church and tearing down the City Hall, which was to be virtually transformed into a new structure dedicated to the use of the first Congress of the United States. The task of designing this building and superintending its erection was intrusted to Major Pierre Charles l'Enfant, a French engineer who had served in the Revolution with great distinction under Baron Steuben, and was to win undying fame by planning the future capital of the nation.[1] The edifice which this distinguished architect located on the site now partially occupied by the

[1] L'Enfant is also credited with having designed a portion of St. Paul's Church.

FEDERAL HALL
(See the descriptive note in the List of Illustrations.)

Sub-Treasury Building and the southern end of Nassau Street was fated to have a very short history, and the only mark it (or its famous predecessor) has left is the curious jog in the northwest corner of Wall and Nassau streets, which marks the turn of the lane or alley bounding its western foothold. But at its inception New York believed it was to be a monument for the ages, and this idea was fairly justified. Certainly no building of such imposing proportions or such artistic design had ever been projected in any American city, and the sum expended on its construction was wholly unprecedented; but the speed with which it was erected and the quarrels between the architect and contractors undoubtedly resulted in bad workmanship and sealed its doom. At its completion, however, it not only realized but surpassed all expectations; for its exterior effect, with its stately arches and classic columns, was exceedingly dignified and imposing, and the interior decorations were the wonder and admiration of all beholders. Indeed, the marble pavement, the painted ceilings, the crimson damask canopies and hangings and handsome furniture, were considered altogether too magnificent by the anti-Federalist press, which saw in them new proofs of the aristocratic tendencies of the new government, and bitterly attacked the distinguished architect, who in the end received little glory and no pay for his services.[1]

It was March 3, 1789, before the Recorder formally tendered the building to Congress,[2] but

[1] The Common Council offered L'Enfant $750 and a grant of city lots (which later became very valuable) and the freedom of the city. He deemed these provisions wholly inadequate, however, and refused to accept them. It is interesting to note that Washington himself evidently found L'Enfant rather difficult during the building of the Federal City, as the national capital was then called, for in one of his letters he writes: "It is much to be regretted, however common the case is, that men who possess talents that fit them for peculiar purposes should almost invariably be under the influence of an untoward disposition or are sottish, idle, or possessed of some other disqualification by which they plague all with whom they are concerned. But I did not expect to have met with such perverseness in Major L'Enfant."

[2] Philadelphia was even then showing jealousy of New York, as appears from the following letter addressed to Recorder Richard Varick:

"Dr. Sir,—It is in my opinion entirely necessary that the Common Council should be convened this day in order to pass an act for appropriating the City Hall to the use of Congress. The act should be published in the papers and notified by yourself, or if you are not well enough, by a committee or member of your board to the Senators and Representatives as they arrive. The Philadelphians are endeavoring to raise some cavils on this point. The thing

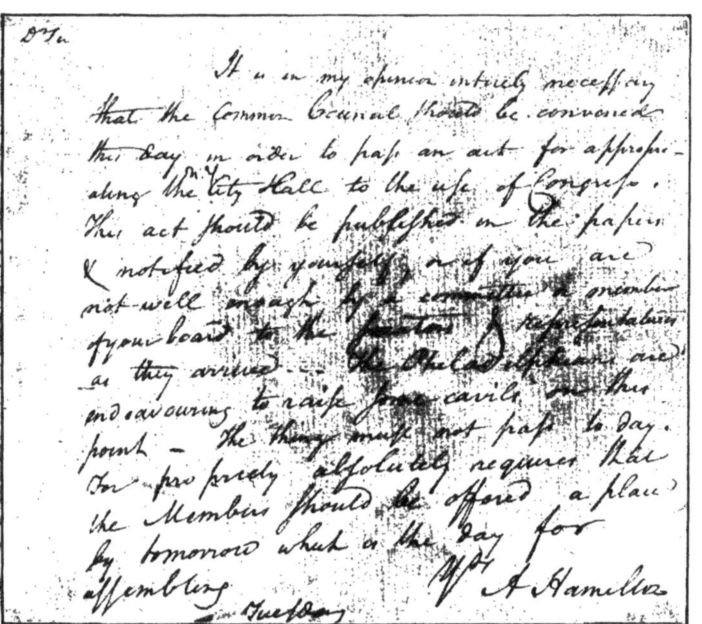

Dr Sir

It is in my opinion intirely necessary that the Common Council should be convened this day in order to pass an act for appropriating the City Hall to the use of Congress. This act should be published in the papers & notified by yourself or if you are not well enough by a committee or member of your board to the [illegible] & representatives as they arrive. The Philadelphians are endeavouring to raise some cavils on this point. The thing must not pass to day. For propriety absolutely requires that the Members should be offered a place by tomorrow which is the day for assembling.

Y^rs A Hamilton

Tuesday

FACSIMILE OF HAMILTON'S HITHERTO UNPUBLISHED LETTER TO RICHARD VARICK, CONCERNING TENDER OF FEDERAL HALL TO CONGRESS

(See the descriptive note in the List of Illustrations.)

very few of the Senators or Representatives had then arrived in the city, and on the day appointed for the opening session there was no quorum in either House. Indeed, it was not until March 30th that the House of Representatives organized, with Frederick Augustus Muhlenberg, of Pennsylvania, in the Speaker's chair, and six more days elapsed before proceedings were initiated in the Senate. On that day, however, the Congress performed its first important duty, and the following morning a brief paragraph in the daily papers announced that a canvass of the electoral vote taken in Federal Hall on Wall Street, April 6, 1789, had resulted in the unanimous election of Washington as first President of the United States, and that John Adams, as recipient of the next highest vote, had been declared Vice-President.

must not pass the day. For propriety absolutely requires that the members should be offered a place by to-morrow which is the day for assembling.

"Yrs A. HAMILTON.

"March 3d, 1789.

"To Richard Varick, Esqr."

XIX

WASHINGTON'S INAUGURATION

FROM that time forward the city was in a flutter of excitement and expectation, and the plans for Washington's reception were discussed on every side. Even the arrival of Adams on April 20th, and his formal installation on the 21st, though attended by highly dignified ceremonies, attracted scarcely any attention, and the news of the ovations which Washington was receiving on his journey from Virginia stimulated the citizens to make New York's welcome worthy of the greatest event in its history. Certainly Wall Street, which had completely recovered its prestige, rose to the occasion, and a brave sight it presented to the crowds which invaded it on the morning of April 23, 1789. From the East River to the rapidly rising Trinity Church flags and banners waved from every building, many of which were also decorated with wreaths of flowers and branches of evergreen; the stairs of Murray's Wharf were carpeted and the rails hung with crimson cloth, and on the pediment at Federal Hall appeared a colossal eagle grasping thirteen arrows and bearing the arms of the United States, which had been recently installed with imposing ceremonies as a finishing-touch to the Congressional building.

Washington arrived at Elizabethtown Point, New Jersey, by nine o'clock on the morning of the 23d, but it was three o'clock in the afternoon before the roar of cannon and clashing of bells announced to the assembled throngs that his magnificent state-barge, manned by thirteen pilots in white uniforms, had been sighted in the East River, and by that time the whole water-front was black with humanity and every roof and window crowded to its utmost capacity. On swept the barge with an accompanying wave of cheers toward the Wall Street wharf, from which Captain Lockyer had made his ignominious exit fifteen years before, and as it swung alongside that historic landing-stage[1] the bands joined the

[1] Among those waiting on the wharf were Governor Clinton, Colonel Morgan Lewis (subsequently Governor of

bells and the cannon in tumultuous welcome. At the same moment the man upon whom all eyes centred rose from his place in the stern of the barge, his plain uniform of buff and blue contrasting sharply with the crimson trappings of the stairs, and as his hand touched the rail the thunderous roar of cheers which greeted him silenced the music and the bells. Then on foot through that seething crowd, declining the carriage provided for his use, Washington passed, amid the acclamations of the assembled thousands, up Wall Street to Queen (Pearl), and thence through that thoroughfare, whose sidewalks were so wonderfully wide that "three persons could walk abreast," to the Franklin House, which had been prepared for his reception.

Thus ended this day of rejoicing, but during all the following week the city was agog with excitement, for from every direction and in all sorts of conveyances visitors kept arriving upon the scene, until every tavern and private dwelling were filled to overflowing, and even the poorest accommodations commanded extravagant pre-

New York), the Mayor and other civil officials, the French and Spanish ambassadors, and many army officers.

WALL STREET IN 1789
(See the descriptive note in the List of Illustrations.)

miums. Meanwhile more Senators and Representatives were making their appearance in Federal Hall, and such men as Oliver Ellsworth, Robert Morris, Samuel Otis, Roger Sherman, James Madison, Jonathan Trumbull, Richard Bland Lee, Elbridge Gerry, William Samuel Johnson, John Page, and others whose names were or were to become famous in the history of the nation, could be daily seen in Wall Street discussing questions of state etiquette and ceremonial and other details of the impending inauguration. Indeed, all the preparations for this great event had not been completed when the day arrived; and when church-bells began summoning the people to their various places of worship for the special services ordained for the morning of April 30, 1789, the congressional committees hastily convened to perfect their arrangements. Meanwhile part of the inaugural procession had formed in front of Federal Hall, and by the time the congregation of the Presbyterian Church issued from their services they found Wall Street ablaze with bunting and festooned with evergreens, and densely packed with spectators who blocked every approach and crowded all the neighboring roofs and windows. It was twelve o'clock, however, before the procession started from the Presidential mansion, and even then the two Houses of Congress were still discussing with some heat and no little confusion the manner in which they should receive Washington and the form in which he should be addressed. Thus another hour slipped by, the dense crowds massed in Wall and Broad streets maintaining perfect order; and finally at one o'clock the head of the procession hove in sight, moving from Great Dock (Pearl) Street into Broad, Captain Stakes and his troopers easily parting the cheering multitude. Within a short distance of Federal Hall the Presidential carriage halted, and Washington, escorted by General Samuel Blatchley Webb (the Beau Brummel of the town), Colonel Nicholas Fish, Colonel William Smith, Colonel Franks, Major Leonard Bleecker, and John R. Livingston, passed through the double line of troopers to the Senate Chamber, followed by the other committees and guests of honor in dignified procession.

Then something very like a panic ensued among those in charge of the arrangements, for

WASHINGTON TAKING OATH AS PRESIDENT IN FEDERAL HALL, ON WALL STREET, APRIL 30, 1789

not until this critical moment was it discovered that an important detail had been completely neglected and that there was no Bible in Federal Hall for the administration of the oath. Chancellor Livingston, however, rose to the occasion, and, hastily despatching a messenger to St. John's (Masonic) Lodge at 115 Broadway, procured the necessary volume, and in a few moments Washington stepped upon the balcony fronting on Wall Street. For an instant he stood in full sight of the assembled multitude, but the wild outburst of cheering which greeted his appearance drove him a step backward, visibly affected. He was dressed in a suit of dark-brown cloth with metal buttons ornamented with eagles, his stockings were white silk, and his shoebuckles silver. At his side he carried a simple steel-hilted dress sword, his powdered hair was worn in the fashion of the times, and close beside him stood Chancellor Robert Livingston, wearing his official robe. Grouped about these two men stood John Adams, George Clinton, Roger Sherman, Baron Steuben, Samuel Otis, Richard Henry Lee, General Arthur St. Clair, and General Knox, and behind them, but not visible from the street, stood members of Congress and other distinguished witnesses.[1]

There was a moment's pause as the company took their positions, and then Samuel Otis, the Secretary of the Senate, carrying a crimson cushion on which rested the hastily borrowed Bible,[2] presented it to the Chancellor, who administered the oath; whereupon Washington kissed the book, and the official proclamation, "Long live George Washington, President of the United States," ended with a thunderous crash of artillery and a renewed burst of cheering.

Such was the day of glory which made New York the capital of the nation, in which for a brief but brilliant period Wall Street was to reign politically and socially supreme.

[1] Alexander Hamilton watched the scene from the window of his house on the opposite side of the street. Washington Irving, then six years of age, was also among the spectators.

[2] This volume is now in the possession of St. John's Lodge, in the Masonic Temple, New York City. According to some authorities its use on this historic occasion was not due to chance, as above set forth, but was deliberately planned.

XX

FROM A FAMOUS DOOR-STEP

NEW YORK was flooded with visitors during the opening year of Washington's administration, and to many of them the cosmopolitan city of thirty thousand inhabitants must have been an astonishing and not altogether agreeable revelation. Certainly its accommodations for transients left something to be desired, for it had never recovered from the effects of the war; its houses and streets were in a lamentable condition, and sore discomfort was apt to be the portion of those who tarried within its gates. Indeed, the only quarter of the national capital which escaped the bitter complaints and scornful descriptions which are recorded at length in the diaries and correspondence of the day was Wall Street. For that well-ordered highway, however, even the most disgruntled strangers often had a word of praise, especially those who viewed it on fine afternoons from Daniel McCormick's door-step. Of course only a favored few were privileged to join the charmed circle of that prince of bachelors, but the guests invited to view the passing throngs from the point of vantage of No. 39,[1] on the south side of the street, witnessed a uniquely interesting scene in the company of people who knew everybody and everything about everybody, and could appraise to a nicety the social standing of all the passers-by. In fact, McCormick's hospitable mansion was the news centre and clearing-house for gossip of the fashionable world of which Wall Street was the centre in the first year of the republic.

Prior to the war the social prestige of the thoroughfare had been second only to Pearl Street,[2] but that famous highway, though it still

[1] This is the old numbering of the street. It is very difficult to locate the corresponding house numbers of the street as it exists to-day, as there was no regularity or sequence in the numbers until late in 1790. No. 5 was, however, apparently at the northwest corner of Wall and William; No. 20 was one of the corners of Wall and Water; No. 32 was near the Coffee-house; No. 44 one door east of the northeast corner of Wall and William, and No. 81 one of the opposite corners.

[2] At this time Pearl Street was only known as such from the present State Street to Broad. From Broad to Wall

boasted the finest houses in the city, had seen its best days, and politically, socially, and historically its rival now reigned supreme. Outwardly the appearance of Wall Street was not as attractive as it had been ten or fifteen years earlier, for few of its splendid shade-trees remained, and that picturesque feature had gone, never to return, for the local authorities had passed an ordinance imposing a penalty of five pounds for planting a tree anywhere below Catharine Street, except in front of a church or other public building, and no one seemed inclined to dispute the wisdom of this law. From an architectural stand-point, however, its condition was vastly improved, for Federal Hall was far more imposing than the old City Hall, and Trinity, which had risen from the ashes of the former building, was altogether more dignified and impressive than its predecessor. Moreover, the whole aspect of the street was more settled, substantial, and uniformly residential than it had previously been, for, with the exception of Baker's Tavern, the headquarters of a club at

it was called Great Dock Street; from Wall to Chatham it was Queen Street. The finest houses were in the Great Dock Street section.

the corner of New Street, a few shops like Adam Prior's, the fashionable caterer at No. 59, and Panton's, the leading jeweller at No. 38, and the public buildings and churches, almost every house from Broadway to Pearl Street was a dignified private dwelling displaying the little oval tin plate which indicated that it had been duly insured in the Mutual Assurance Company against fire.

It was not the Wall Street of brick and stone, however, which fascinated those who viewed it on gala days from Daniel McCormick's high door-step. What interested them was the panorama of life, the constantly changing figures, the gay colors, the quaint characters, the men of mark, the fashions and foibles—all the human elements of the miniature Vanity Fair that strutted and plumed itself on the fashionable promenade through which there swirls to-day a hurrying stream of life. Here approached a remarkable old gentleman gowned in a black clerical robe and bands, and wearing a white buzz wig, a three-cornered hat, and silver shoebuckles, who threaded his way through the crowd, representing all the city could boast of worth, wit, and cult-

WALL STREET THE CENTRE OF FASHION, 1789
(See the descriptive note in the List of Illustrations)

ure, with a masterful clumping of his gold-headed cane upon the pavement, and the most ceremonious of salutations to right and to left. Any one of McCormick's coterie could inform the uninitiated that this was the Reverend Dr. John Rodgers, of the Presbyterian Church, a patriot it well became one to know, and a gentleman of such majestic dignity that he seldom appeared in public without his official robes, and rumor had it that he and his wife exchanged a formal bow and a deep courtesy each night when they retired. Here, too, appeared another gentleman of the old school in a scarlet coat and cocked hat, enthroned on the cushions of a quaint pony-phaeton, from which he surveyed the moving throng with a proprietary air, his hands resting proudly upon his massive cane, for Washington's physician, Dr. John Bard, was the fashionable doctor of his day, and he could count his patients by the dozen on Wall Street when society took the air. The handsome man whom both of these old gentlemen distinguished with particularly gracious bows was Sir John Temple, whose too great "inclination toward the American cause" had lost him the Lieutenant-Governorship of New Hampshire, but made him the most popular of British consul-generals.[1] Indeed, Sir John was New York's official host, for he invariably welcomed every distinguished arrival in the city with a call of ceremony, and no one in the community was more generally admired.

Logically it should have been the French and not the English representative who found favor with the public in those days, but the observer who noted the Marquis de Moustier's red-heeled shoes and gold ear-rings in the crowd and inquired concerning their owner would learn that His Highness was not in high favor with the elect, and that his sister, Madame la Marquise de Brienne, the lady greeting the passers-by from her sedan-chair, was courted for her entertainments and unmercifully ridiculed behind her back. It must be admitted, however, that the Marquis had been guilty of even worse manners than his sister's guests, for if the gossips at Mc-

[1] Sir John Temple (who married Miss Bowdoin of Massachusetts), died in New York and was buried in St. Paul's church-yard. The tablet erected to his memory still adorns the church.

Cormick's could be believed he had once actually brought his own cook to Vice-President Adams's house and caused private dishes to be served to him at his host's table, coolly remarking that he had had some experience with bad dinners in New York and could not afford to repeat it.

Probably none of these distinguished gentlemen would have been recognized by a stranger, but there were faces in the moving throng which were familiar beyond the confines of New York. For instance, almost every Virginian would have been able to identify Cyrus Griffin, the President of Congress, and Lady Christiana, his wife, who were well known in that State; and Thomas Jefferson, lately returned from the court of Versailles, in his red waistcoat and breeches, was quite as familiar to his compatriots as he was to many of the leaders in the city's social whirl. Here, too, the observer could note John Hancock, whose name was writ large on the historic scroll, and Aaron Burr, the Attorney-General, conspicuous for the cordiality with which he was greeted upon every hand, particularly by the ladies, among whom he always found exceptional favor; and Baron Steuben, the disciplinary genius of Valley Forge, now president of the Society of the Cincinnati; and Colonel John Trumbull, the portrait-painter, who had learned his art under Benjamin West; and Commodore Paul Jones, whom society preferred to call the Chevalier. There were many interesting rumors in circulation about the doughty little Commodore in those days, of which the story that he and Captain Landais had had an exciting encounter was on everybody's tongue. Landais was the naval officer who was credited with having displayed more discretion than valor, and more prudence than discretion, in the battle between the *Bon Homme Richard* and the *Serapis*. In fact, according to Jones's story, the Frenchman had remained safely out of range during most of that engagement, and when he had at last ventured near enough to be of service he had lost his head and raked the *Bon Homme Richard* instead of his adversary, after which masterly performance he had again sought and held the horizon line until the day was won. Landais denied these charges to his dying day, but a court of inquiry had found him guilty on other grounds, and from that moment the world was scarcely

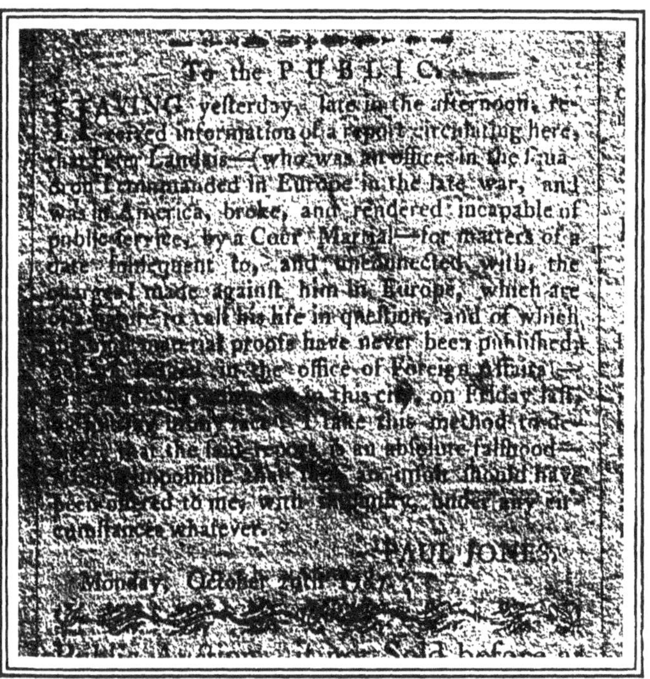

To the PUBLIC.

HAVING yesterday, late in the afternoon, received information of a report circulating here, that Peter Landais—(who was an officer in the squadron I commanded in Europe in the late war, and was in America, broke, and rendered incapable of public service, by a Court Martial—for matters of a date subsequent to, and unconnected with, the charges I made against him in Europe, which are of a nature to call his life in question, and of which [illegible] material proofs have never been published, [illegible] in the office of Foreign Affairs— [illegible] in this city, on Friday last, [illegible] I take this method to declare [illegible] the said report is an absolute falsehood— [illegible] impossible that [illegible] should have been offered to me, with [illegible], under any circumstances whatever.

PAUL JONES.

Monday, October 2[illegible] 17[illegible].

CARD FROM PAUL JONES PUBLISHED IN "NEW YORK PACKET"
(See the descriptive note in the List of Illustrations.)

wide enough to hold him and his accuser. Therefore when it was rumored that he had confronted Jones on Water Street and spat upon the sidewalk, declaring, with great delicacy, that his defamer might regard the pavement as his face, there were those who thought the story characteristic of the Frenchman's histrionic instinct, but there were very few who believed that he could have roused his courage to the sticking-point and lived to tell the tale. Nevertheless, somebody must have credited the yarn, for Jones's spirited denial was printed over his own signature in a leading paper,[1] and the gossips continued to whisper it, glancing apprehensively over their shoulders, for many a long day after. There were others among the passing pedestrians, however, of whom the gossips had a less cautious word. For instance, Mrs. General Knox, decidedly plumper and altogether less romantic-looking than she was at the beginning of the war, when she eloped with Henry Knox (the Boston bookseller, turned artillerist), because her loyalist father would not countenance a rebel son-in-law. But it was not the stout-hearted young bride who accompanied

[1] N. Y. *Packet*, October 29, 1787.

her husband on his perilous campaigns and lightened their hardships and won Washington's regard whom the gossips celebrated, but rather the stout-waisted matron who was the Mrs. Malaprop of their circle and at whose original remarks society twittered, not too politely, behind its well-drilled fans.

XXI

FASHIONS AND NOTABLES

IT was a fashionably attired company which filled the narrow sidewalks, the blue coats, variously colored waistcoats, and knee breeches of the men combining with the gay silks and satins affected by the women to lend brightness and an air of festivity to the scene. Indeed, some of the men arrayed themselves much more conspicuously than the women; for John Ramage, the Irish miniature-painter, whose studio was on William Street, not far from Wall, was accustomed to join the promenade attired in a scarlet coat with mother-of-pearl buttons, a white silk waistcoat embroidered with colored flowers, black satin breeches, with paste knee-buckles, white silk stockings, and a small cocked hat perched on his curled and powdered hair. Contrasted with this gorgeous display the description of the latest Parisian novelty in favor with the fair sex suggests extreme simplicity. This creation consisted of "a perriot and petticoat, both made of the same gray striped silk, trimmed all around with gauze cut in points, in the manner of Herrisons which were made of ribbons or Italian gauze." With this was worn "a large gauze handkerchief with four satin stripes round its border two very broad and the others less, the handkerchief itself being an ell and a half square, and for head-dress a plain gauze cap made in the form of those worn by the elders or ancients in the nunneries."[1] Not all the ladies, however, exhibited such quiet tastes, for here and there were to be seen "celestial blues" and "caracos and petticoats of Indian taffaty" and "perriots with two collars, one yellow and one white"; and "blue satin shoes with rose-colored rosettes," and among the wearers of this brilliant raiment were numbered all the social leaders of their day. Here sauntered Mr. and Mrs. John Watts, the latter better known as Lady Mary (for the élite of the republican court still scrupulously accorded their titles to women of rank), and Assistant Secretary of the Treasury William Duer with his wife,

[1] N. Y. *Gazette*, May 15, 1789.

the Lady Kitty of her day; and Colonel and Mrs. Alexander Hamilton, and Senator Ralph Izard and his lady, who was Miss De Lancey of New York, and many another couple whose names were widely known.

Indeed, Wall Street might have called the roll of the socially elect from Mrs. John Jay's famous list of guests almost any summer afternoon, and reported all present or accounted for; for many of the most prominent families, such as the Winthrops, the Jaunceys, the Verplancks, and the Ludlows, still lived on the highway, and several of the most distinguished members of Congress, such as Richard Basset, Benjamin Contee, Thomas Sumpter, Elias Boudinot, Lambert Cadwallader, and Richard Bland Lee, dated from Mrs. Lloyd Daubeney's[1] fashionable boarding-house. In fact, this exclusive establishment made almost every visitor of distinction a temporary resident of Wall Street, and fortunate indeed were those who secured its accommodations, for

[1] Mrs. Lloyd Daubeney, whose maiden name was Mary Coventry, came of good family. She was related to the fifth Earl of Coventry. The family held Pew 14 in Trinity for many years. (Barrett's *Old Merchants of New York*, vol. iv.).

the Merchants' Coffee-house[1] was no longer in its prime, and Fraunces's Tavern was not a desirable hostelry after its proprietor, Black Sam, assumed charge of the Presidential ménage. There was, however, another refuge for the wayfarer at No. 81 (one of the southerly corners of Wall and William), and this private hostelry, which rejoiced in the plebeian name of Huck's, sheltered Daniel Huger, Thomas Tudor Tucker, Edanus Burke, and other Congressional representatives from the South.

From McCormick's hospitable door-step the visitor could likewise descry the residences of most of the exponents of New York's official life. At the northwest corner of Wall and William streets lived Van Berckel, the minister from Holland; at No. 5, Samuel Otis, the Secretary of the Senate; at No. 8, the Postmaster, William Bedlow; at No. 13, John Lawrence, the first Congressman from New York city, who later became a judge and a United States Senator; at No. 44,

[1] Though this historic hostelry, then known as Bradford's, was passing, it was utilized by the Marine Society, the New York Hospital, the Order of Cincinnati, St. John's Masonic Lodge No. 2, and other notable organizations for their early meetings.

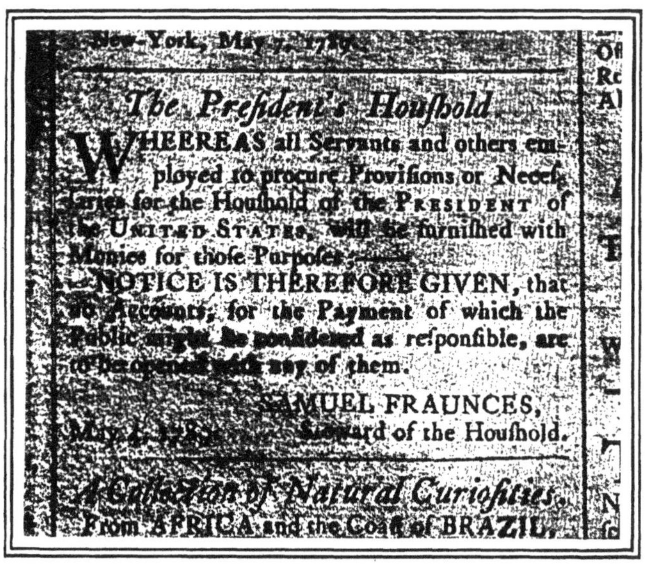

New-York, May 7, 1789.

The President's Houshold.

WHEREAS all Servants and others employed to procure Provisions or Necessaries for the Houshold of the PRESIDENT of the UNITED STATES, will be furnished with Monies for those Purposes:——

NOTICE IS THEREFORE GIVEN, that no Accounts, for the Payment of which the Public might be considered as responsible, are to be opened with any of them.

SAMUEL FRAUNCES,

May 4, 1789. Steward of the Houshold.

A Collection of Natural Curiosities,

From AFRICA and the Coast of BRAZIL,

A WARNING BY WASHINGTON'S STEWARD

(See the descriptive note in the List of Illustrations.)

General John Lamb, the first Collector of the Port; at No. 52, Richard Varick, the Mayor; at No. 58, Alexander Hamilton, the Secretary of the Treasury; at No. 60, William Irvin, the Commissioner of Accounts; at No. 64, James Culbertson, the High Constable; while at other points lived the Dennings, the Wilkes, the Pintards, the Edgars, and other prominent New-Yorkers of their day.

Such were some of the men and women who lived and moved and had their being in Wall Street, and the visitors who chanced to be present on one of the occasions when Washington attended Congress in his state-coach saw the highway at its best. It was a wonderful creation, that canary-colored Presidential chariot,[1] with its ornamental crests and its decorations of gilded nymphs and cupids, but Washington doubtless often wished that it was a trifle less conspicuous as he rumbled over the stones of Wall Street to Federal Hall. Indeed, there was probably noth-

[1] Part of this historic vehicle was later cut into boxes and sold at a church fair, and the seat and steps turned into garden ornaments by the unimaginative individuals who obtained possession of it.

ing in his many vexatious official duties which he so thoroughly disliked as making this public exhibition of himself, despite the anti-Federalist sneers at his aristocratic tastes and tendencies. But the general public unquestionably enjoyed the spectacle, and when the ceremonial carriage, with a gorgeous coachman on its throne-like box, and a footman standing behind, and its six horses with their gay trappings and "painted" hoofs, swung into view, preceded by uniformed outriders and followed by an accompanying cavalcade, all the local world was there to see.

As a matter of fact, Wall Street saw very little of the President during his official residence in New York. Of course he attended the so-called inauguration ball, which was held on May 7, 1789, at the City Assembly Rooms on Broadway, just around the corner of Wall, where he danced two cotillons and perhaps a minuet, of which event Jefferson has left a description that would do credit to the most imaginative sensation-monger of the modern press. The Executive likewise honored the grand affair at the French Embassy, where those who took part in the quadrilles were attired in gorgeous costumes symbolical of America and France and the festivities "were at their height at ten o'clock"; but there is very little evidence of his having been present at the other distinguished routs and entertainments of the day.[1] Nor did he grace the dinners for which Wall Street was famous in the years of its social glory, when many a distinguished company was gathered around its hospitable boards. This was partially due to the death of his mother, which occurred during the year, and to his own ill-health; but the difficulty of making distinctions was mainly responsible for his absence, and even then one of his letters shows that he and his wife never had an opportunity of dining alone. In fact, he had not been long in town before the necessity of adopting some general rules as to what invitations he would give or accept became apparent, and Hamilton[2] drew a simple plan regulating the Presidential entertainments, receptions, dinners, visits, etc., which,

[1] There were no less than three dancing - schools in the immediate vicinity of Wall Street at this time.

[2] Washington appears to have drawn up a set of questions concerning his official conduct and etiquette, and submitted them to both Hamilton and Adams. (McMaster's *History of the People of the United States*, vol. i., p. 564; *N. Y. Journal*, May 7, 1789.)

with very slight modifications, has governed every occupant of the White House to the present day. Thus the etiquette of the Executive Mansion may fairly be said to have originated in Wall Street, where Hamilton and his fair lady were famed for their hospitality.

At their table assembled such men as Jefferson, Knox, Adams, Jay, Madison, and other prominent statesmen, and the sentiments pledged on those occasions were eagerly awaited and variously interpreted, for more than one important event in the history of the nation had its inception at these little Wall Street dinners.[1] Indeed, the political leaders usually divulged their policies and platforms on such occasions through the medium of carefully worded toasts, and not all of them were as plain and pointed as that offered at the dinner of the General Society of Mechanics and Tradesmen, which suggested "*A cobweb pair of breeches, a porcupine saddle, a hard-trotting horse, and a long journey for all the enemies of liberty!*" Hamilton was not the only resident of the street

[1] It was at a dinner at Jefferson's house that the bargain was struck whereby the national capital was located at Washington.

who was noted for entertainments of this sort, for Van Berckel, the minister from Holland, kept open house at the old Marston mansion on the northwest corner of Wall and William, and here all the members of the Diplomatic Corps with their wives and families were wined and dined informally and in state, and Daniel McCormick's bachelor banquets at No. 39 were justly the talk of the town. Of course there was nothing magnificent or luxurious in these entertainments. New York was still a provincial town of comparatively simple tastes, and there was nowhere any display of wealth. Society depended for its importance upon the personal qualities of its members, and in the heart of the capital there was gathered from all parts of the country a company which gave it a tone and distinction impossible under modern conditions.

XXII

THE PASSING OF NATIONAL HONORS

BRILLIANT as its social record had become, Wall Street had not in the mean time lost anything of its official dignity and had materially added to its historic laurels. On March 25, 1790, Trinity was duly consecrated, and, with a canopied pew set apart for the President and another specially reserved for the Governor, it bade fair to continue its long tradition as the official place of worship.

Meanwhile within the halls of Congress business of vital importance to the nation had been transacted. On April 7, 1789, a committee was appointed by the Senate to frame a bill for the judicial courts of the United States, and on June 12th of that year Richard Henry Lee reported the measures drawn by Oliver Ellsworth, of Connecticut, which brought into existence the most powerful tribunal known to the history of the law.

Indeed, it was on September 24, 1789, in Federal Hall, at the corner of Wall and Nassau streets, that Washington performed the most important act of his administrative career, for on that day he signed the measure creating the Supreme Court of the United States. Certainly nothing ordained by Congress before or since that day has had so profound an effect upon American history as the creation of that mighty tribunal, and from the little court-house on the other side of Wall Street came two of its first judges—John Jay and Brockholst Livingston.

In February, 1790, another significant event occurred in Federal Hall, for a petition presented by the Quakers praying for the abolition of slavery led to a sharp debate, and the next day the last word of advice which Franklin was destined to offer his countrymen was received in the form of a memorial signed by him as president of the Pennsylvanian Society for Promoting the Abolition of Slavery. The discussion on this subject lasted for more than a month, and even at that early date there were muttered threats of secession in the air. It was not the slavery question, however, which then suggested the dissolution of the

Union, but rather Hamilton's policy for the assumption of the State debts, which, to the State-rights men, seemed to foreshadow the extinction of all local sovereignty. So bitter was the feeling against the Federal plan that Hamilton was forced to offer great concessions to carry his point, and the compromise he negotiated disposed of New York as the permanent national capital.

Meanwhile the fates had long been combining to strip the city of its official honors, for an extraordinarily hot summer and a bitter winter had prejudiced all the visiting members of Congress and intensified the local jealousy and resentment of less favored communities, all of which were vigorously contending for possession of the prize. Such was the situation when Hamilton made his famous bargain with Jefferson by which the Potomac was selected as the site of the future capital, Philadelphia given a lease of power for ten years, and the national government authorized to assume the debts of the several States. The part of this compromise which divested New York of its official character took the form of an Act of Congress which was signed by Washington on July 16, 1790, but Wall Street was privileged

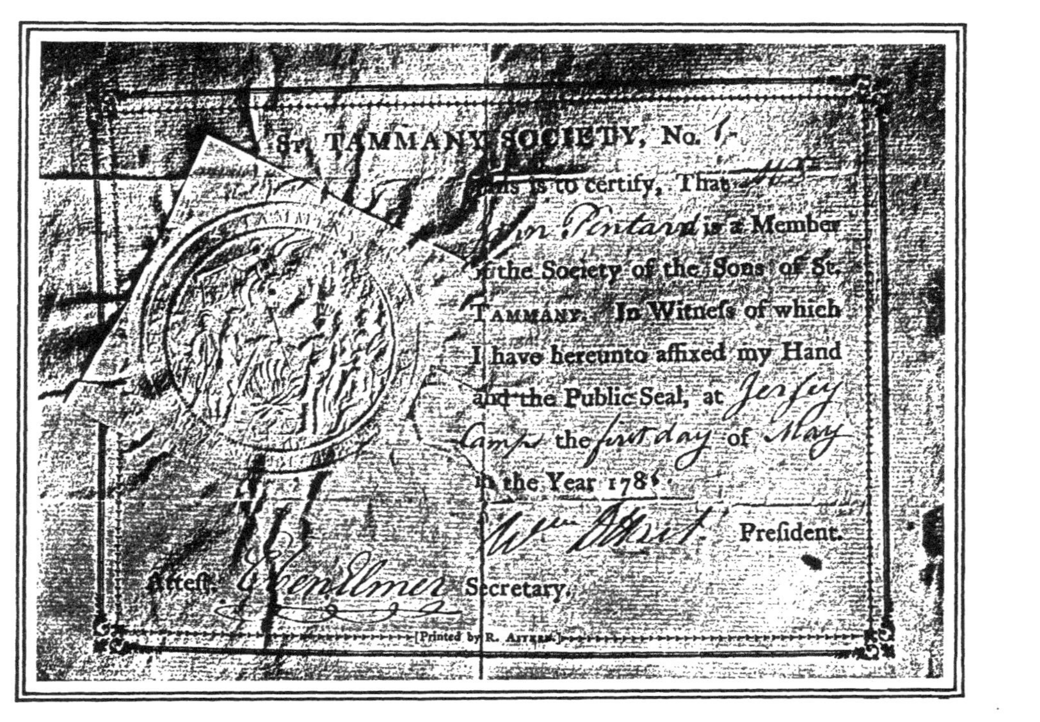

ST. TAMMANY SOCIETY, No. 1

This is to certify, That

Pintard is a Member of the Society of the Sons of St. TAMMANY. In Witness of which I have hereunto affixed my Hand and the Public Seal, at Jersey Camp the first day of May in the Year 178

President.

Attest. Secretary.

[Printed by R. AITKEN.]

ONE OF THE EARLIEST CERTIFICATES OF MEMBERSHIP IN TAMMANY

(See the descriptive note in the List of Illustrations.)

to witness one more interesting ceremony before it went into effect.

Late in that month Colonel Marinus Willett, who had been in the South negotiating a treaty of peace with the Creek Indians, returned to New York, bringing with him the chief and twenty-eight warriors of the tribe. At every stopping-place on their journey Colonel Willett and his party had been received with great courtesy and hospitality, and on their arrival in New York they were met and welcomed by a new society whose members donned bucktails and otherwise arrayed themselves in full Indian costume, and, assuming entire charge of the proceedings, conducted the puzzled redskins to Federal Hall.

Such was the first public appearance of Tammany, organized in 1789 to spread "*the smile of charity, the chain of friendship, and the flame of liberty, and in general whatever may tend to perpetuate the love of freedom or the political advantage of this country.*" None of those worthy objects would seem to have called the society into the field as the self-appointed reception committee to the visiting Creek Indians, but the occasion undoubtedly served to bring the organization into prominence, and under its auspices the proceedings, though smacking somewhat of burlesque, were apparently conducted to every one's satisfaction. Indeed, the Society of the Cincinnati, whose aristocratic pretensions unquestionably called St. Tammany into the field, fraternized with its rival on this occasion, and on July 27, 1790, the President made his last official visit to Wall Street in his ornate coach, with all the trappings of dignity, to sign a treaty with the Indians and pass the pipe of peace.

It was August 12th when Congress adjourned, and on the 30th Washington was conveyed across the North River in the same magnificent barge that had brought him to the city which he was never to see again, and almost with his departure changes were begun in Wall Street which were to give it a new place in a very different phase of history.

New-York City Lottery.

SCHEME *of a* LOTTERY, *for the purpose of raising* Seven Thousand Five Hundred Pounds, *agreeable to an Act of the* LEGISLATURE *of the State of* NEW-YORK, *passed 8th February*, 1790.

SCHEME.

1 *Prize of*	£. 3000	-	£. 3000
2 -	1000	-	2000
3 -	500	-	1500
10 -	200	-	2000
30 -	100	-	3000
50 -	50	-	2500
120 -	20	-	2400
180 -	10	-	1800
7950 -	4	-	31800

8346 *Prizes.*
16654 *Blanks.* } 25,000 Tickets, at 40s. each, - - - - £. 50000

Subject to a deduction of 15 per Cent.

THE object of this LOTTERY being to raise a part of the sum advanced by the Corporation for repairing and enlarging the CITY-HALL, for the accommodation of CONGRESS, which does so much honor to the Architect, as well as credit to the City. The Managers presume, that their Fellow-Citizens will cheerfully concur in promoting the sale of Tickets, especially, as the success of this Lottery will relieve them from a Tax, which must otherwise be laid to reimburse the Corporation.

The above SCHEME is calculated in a manner very beneficial to Adventurers, there not being *two Blanks to a Prize.*

The Lottery is intended to commence drawing on the *first Monday in August next*, or sooner if filled, of which timely notice will be given. A list of the fortunate numbers will be published at the expiration of the drawing.

Tickets are to be sold by the subscribers, who are appointed Managers by the Corporation.

ISAAC STOUTENBURGH,
PETER T. CURTENIUS,
ABRAHAM HERRING,
JOHN PINTARD.

New-York, *March* 6, 1790.

LOTTERY SCHEME TO PAY FOR FEDERAL HALL
(See the descriptive note in the List of Illustrations)

XXIII

THE DAWN OF A NEW ERA

DOWN by the Battery the building designed for the Executive Mansion was nearing completion, and up on Wall Street Federal Hall, dedicated to the use of Congress, was almost paid for; but the President had gone never to return, and Philadelphia had become the national capital. The situation was disappointing, humiliating, and, in view of the futile preparations, even ludicrous, but New York wasted no time in idle lamentation. Socially and politically its year and a half of glory as the seat of the national government had given it a pleasant prestige, but the thoughts and ambitions of its people were concerned with more material advantages. Moreover, it still remained the capital of the State, and with the legislature and the municipal authorities quartered in the City Hall, Wall Street was not wholly divested of political importance.

Indeed, within five months after Congress abandoned it, the highway witnessed an event profoundly affecting the history of the nation, for in the building still commonly known as Federal Hall, on January 3, 1791, Aaron Burr was elected to a seat in the United States Senate, and from that moment a new and decidedly disturbing factor was injected into all political calculations.

The exact causes of Burr's sudden elevation to power have never been satisfactorily determined, but it is possible that he was, even then, cultivating the friendship of Tammany, over which he subsequently exerted a commanding influence, and it may well be that the approval of some of its prominent members contributed to his success. Officially the society had not as yet evinced any direct interest in politics, but there is evidence that its leaders were already manœuvring for a political opening, and the advice of its patron saint to the children of "the second tribe" was deeply significant of coming events. "*The tiger affords a useful lesson for you,*" observed that legendary sage. "*The exceeding agility of this creature, the extraordinary quickness of his sight, and, above all, his discriminating power in the dark, teach you to be stirring and active in your respective callings; to look sharp to every engagement you enter into, and to let neither misty days nor stormy nights make you lose sight of the worthy object of your pursuit.*" [1]

Probably this admonition had no controlling influence upon the founders of the organization, but its activities had already brought it into prominence, and it early obtained a foothold in the City Hall for the public-spirited purpose of establishing a Museum of American History.[2] Thus Wall Street, which had housed the first public library known to the city, became the repository of one of the earliest collections of historic relics assembled in the country, and not many years later it witnessed the founding of the New York Historical Society, whose early meetings were held in the picture-room of the City

[1] Chief Tammany is supposed to have divided his people into thirteen tribes, each of which had a totem or symbol of clanship in the form of some animal whose virtues the chief recommended to their notice. The New York institution claims identification with the second tribe.—Drake, *History of the Tammany Society.*

[2] This collection was later moved to a house on the south side of the street, and was subsequently scattered, part of it passing into the possession of P. T. Barnum of circus fame.

Hall. Meanwhile other societies secured accommodations under the same roof, which thus became the headquarters of the Medical Society, the St. Cæcilia, the Uranium, and similar organizations, while toward the other end of the historic highway a group of auctioneering firms were quietly moulding its future. As a matter of fact, however, Wall Street's destiny had been determined at that little dinner at Jefferson's house, where Hamilton had sold New York's political birthright to insure the assumption of the State debts, for most of the public stock[1] which the Treasury issued to finance its plan was marketed through the auctioneering establishments located at the eastern end of the still fashionable thoroughfare. Indeed, the first "stock-exchange" known to the city opened at No. 22[2] about the first of March, 1792, was a direct effort on the part of the auctioneers to control this business, and it is a curious fact that two of the men associated in this enterprise, McEvers and Pintard, represent-

[1] This was virtually the same as the modern government bonds.

[2] The street numbers used at this period practically correspond to those of the present day.

ed families closely identified with Wall Street's previous history.

No marked alteration had yet occurred in the appearance of the street, but under one of the few shade-trees[1] which had escaped destruction during the Revolution there now gathered daily a small group of men who acted as brokers in the purchase and sale of the public stock, and their presence gradually effected a change in the character of the quiet residential neighborhood. Moreover, it was soon apparent that these men had determined to maintain the foothold they had acquired, for they were quick to resent the combination of the auctioneers which threatened to drive them from the field, and lost no time in declaring war against the allied firms. At a meeting held in Corre's Hotel on March 21, 1792, they resolved to have no dealings with the monopolists, and on March 17th of the same year they subscribed to a written memorandum agreeing upon a definite commission and undertaking to give each other preference in all brokerage transactions.

[1] A buttonwood which stood in front of Nos. 68–70 Wall Street.

Such was the origin of the New York Stock-Exchange, but there was no immediate attempt to effect a permanent organization, and for some years the trading conducted under the old button-wood-tree was almost entirely confined to the marketing of the public stock.

Meanwhile the first notable break from its ancient traditions was occurring at the eastern end of the highway, for the Merchants' Coffee-house was nearing the close of its distinguished career, and in 1793 it was practically eclipsed by a rival establishment housed in a modern structure erected by subscription,[1] on the Tontine plan, at the northwest corner of Wall and Water streets. This building, known as the Tontine Coffee-house, was conducted not only as an inn, but also as a merchants' exchange, and is fairly entitled to rank among the first office buildings known to the city, which then numbered thirty-five thousand inhabitants. Here in 1793 the associated brokers established their first official headquarters, and before long it became the storm centre of the absurd political agitation

[1] Two hundred and three persons contributed $200 apiece to this enterprise.

which then convulsed the entire city, for in default of a better issue at that time the community ranged itself on either side of the impending struggle between France and England, and the local elections were fiercely contested by the partisans of those countries, without the slightest regard to any other question. Provincial and undignified as such a contest was, party feeling ran high in 1793, and it was at this juncture that Wall Street was drawn into the inglorious fray.

XXIV

POLITICS AND BROKERAGE

THE trouble began at the Tontine Coffee-house, where the zealous champions of France raised a liberty-cap, which the English contingent immediately threatened to remove. The French party thereupon set a guard over the building and defied their opponents, the supporters of each side rushed to the rescue, and Wall Street was soon thronged with hundreds of angry men. Neither faction, however, seemed inclined to take the initiative, and after daring and double-daring each other with puerile provocations to the point of exhaustion, the farcical contest ended.

About this time Citizen Bompard, a French naval officer, commanding the war-ship *L'Ambuscade*, arrived in the port, and taunts and defiances were soon flying thick and fast over the glasses of the mettlesome sons of the sea who frequented the Tontine. Finally the Master of a United States revenue-cutter arrived on the scene bearing a message from Captain Courtney, of his Majesty's frigate *Boston*, challenging the French commander to a naval duel. This extraordinary communication was actually spread upon the books of the Coffee-house,[1] and when Courtney appeared in the town Citizen Bompard and he soon ran foul of each other. Thereupon the preliminaries were quickly arranged, and, sailing out of the harbor, the two valiant gentlemen pummelled each other with cannon for several hours, within hearing but just out of sight of the cheering throngs gathered on the neighboring hills.[2]

A year later the Franco-British controversy was still raging, and had it then been known that Jay had negotiated his famous treaty with England his candidacy for the Governorship would have been seriously affected. He was, however. safely inaugurated in the City Hall, July 1, 1795, and the contents of the treaty did not become

[1] *Pennsylvania Gazette*, July 31, 1793.

[2] This remarkable contest took place near Sandy Hook. The English commander was killed. Some enterprising mariners actually advertised that they would take passengers down to Sandy Hook to see the fight. (*American Daily Advertiser*, August 1, 1793.)

public until the following day. The moment its provisions were understood, however, the partisans of France raised a howl of indignation, and, shrieking every charge against the statesman which ignorance and malice could invent, called mass-meetings to demand his repudiation at the hands of the Senate. One of these meetings was scheduled for Wall Street, and in front of the City Hall a turbulent throng assembled. There was, however, a strong anti-French contingent represented in the crowd, and when efforts were made to adjourn the proceedings a scene of wild confusion followed. Richard Varick and Brockholst Livingston attempted to address the mob, but were howled down, and then Alexander Hamilton, mounting the steps of his house on the corner of Wall and Broad streets, tried to gain a hearing. The mob, however, was in no mood to listen to a man whom it regarded as a notorious champion of England, and stones were soon flying through the air. "*If you employ such striking arguments, I must retire*," announced the orator, and in a few moments the rabble swept by him toward the Government House on Bowling Green, where Jay was violently denounced, the rejection of his treaty demanded, and a copy of it burned in front of the official residence. Neither Washington nor the Senate, however, paid the slightest attention to these noisy demonstrations, and the ratification of Jay's negotiation which followed was soon justified by the event. Indeed, within a few years some of the very men, whose wild-eyed enthusiasm for France suggested a religious frenzy, were shrieking maledictions against that country and urging the administration to make an immediate declaration of war against her. In the mean time, however, Jay did not add to his popularity, for in 1796 he incurred the displeasure of Tammany by declining to honor the anniversary of the society by ordering a display of flags—a precedent which has not protected other incumbents of the City Hall from similar outbursts of wrath.

The volume of business transacted by the brokers during these turbulent years was not very great, and the dealings were still limited to a few stocks, but certain memoranda contained in the note-book of one of the small group who continued to assemble under the buttonwood-tree in 1793 show that some phases of the brokerage business were much the same in the eighteenth century as they are in the twentieth. For instance, in the note-book above mentioned, under date of February 13, 1795, this entry has survived: "*I bet G. McEvers* 10 *Dollars to* 5 *Dollars that there would not be* 3000 *votes taken at the ensuing election for Governor in the City and County of New York.*" And again: "*Feby.* 17, 1795, *I bet Robert Cocks, Sr., a pair of satin breeches that Jay would be elected Governor by a majority of* 500 *or more.*"

The writer of these engagements was evidently doing a brisk business in the winter of 1795, but Jay was almost the last Federalist upon whose success at the polls it would have been safe to count for a pair of silk breeches or any other advantage, for Burr's political star was in the ascendant, and Tammany was preparing to supply him with what Hamilton termed his "myrmidons" and Theodosia Burr called "recruits for the Tenth Legion."

The Federalists were, however, still sufficiently intrenched in power to prevent their opponents from obtaining a charter for any rival to the Bank of New York, which had been organized with Hamilton's assistance, and was, in 1798, located in a building erected on the site of the McEvers mansion at the northeast corner of Wall and William streets.[1] During its existence of fourteen years this corporation had acquired virtual monopoly of the local banking business, and as New York was rapidly increasing in population, the advantage of the facilities afforded by the Federal institution became a valuable political asset. Indeed, it was openly charged that none but Federalist sympathizers could obtain accommodations at its hands, and in the legislature every effort to place a competitor in the field was summarily blocked. In 1799, however, Burr appeared upon the scene as the sponsor for a company whose ostensible business was the improvement of New York's water-supply. In view of the recent epidemics, which were generally attributed to bad water, the projectors of this public-spirited enterprise were promptly accorded the necessary charter, authorizing a capital of two million dollars, and providing that any surplus not needed for the immediate prosecution of the business "*might be employed in any way not*

[1] See inscription on present building No. 48 Wall Street.

inconsistent with the laws and Constitution of the United States, or of the State of New York."

This legislative "joker" did not entirely escape notice, but in the face of the plausible explanations offered by the company's counsel and the honest anxiety of the authorities concerning the public health it practically met with no objection. Indeed, it must have been difficult for Burr and his adherents to conceal their joy when they perceived the ease with which they were to accomplish their ends, but their secret was well kept, and not until the Manhattan Company was safely established at No. 23 Wall Street, employing its "surplus capital" *in the banking business*, did the Federalists discover that their enemies had stolen a march on them, and were in a position from which they could not be dislodged. From this time forward the business of chartering banks played an important part in the sessions of the legislature, and methods were employed to obtain the coveted privileges which would scandalize the most hardened of modern corruptionists; but within a few years the Merchants',[1] the

[1] The Merchants' was located at No. 25, the United States at No. 38, and the Mechanics' at No. 16 Wall Street.

Mechanics', and the United States Bank were incorporated, and all of them made their headquarters on Wall Street.

Less than ten years elapsed between the retirement of Congress and the establishment of the Manhattan Company, but during that time the population of the city had increased from thirty-five to sixty thousand people, and the character of its historic highway was being gradually transformed. Indeed, the advance-guard of fashion had already begun to move up to Park Row at the opening of the nineteenth century, and the gaps caused by this migration were quickly occupied by the pioneers of finance. Business was still conducted on a very modest scale, however, and for some years the thoroughfare maintained a residential aspect. Fashion had never favored the neighborhood of the Tontine Coffee-house, and such private houses as there were in that vicinity fell an easy prey to the commercial invasion, but between Pearl Street and Broadway every foot of territory was contested, the private dwellings surrendering only one by one. Even

The first two were incorporated in 1805, and the last in 1810.

then those that capitulated often managed to conceal the fact until long after the event, for the days of conspicuous advertising had not yet arrived, and the new tenants frequently preferred to make no alteration in the premises. Here and there a sign was displayed, and at a few points the oldest houses were replaced by modern structures, such as that of the Bank of New York, but save in these particulars there was as yet little evidence of the coming transformation.

Such was the aspect of the street on the morning of July 11, 1804, when a bulletin, displayed on the Tontine Coffee-house, attracted the attention of the earliest arrivals, and in a few moments messengers were speeding through the city carrying the startling news that Hamilton and Burr had met in a duel, and that the former lay at the point of death. From that moment business was practically suspended, and all day long great throngs gathered before the Coffee-house, watching the bulletins which reported the famous statesman's brief struggle for life. The end was announced on the afternoon of the 12th, and on Saturday, the 14th, Wall Street witnessed the most impressive funeral pageant known to the

TRINITY CHURCH IN 1804
(See the descriptive note in the List of Illustrations.)

history of the city. Every window and roof was crowded with mourners as the body was borne to Trinity, and the junction of Wall Street and Broadway was lined with troops, the soldiers leaning their cheeks against the butts of their inverted rifles in an attitude of grief. Between their ranks passed the procession, which included the Governor, the Mayor, the judges, members of Congress, foreign ministers, representatives of Tammany, the Cincinnati, St. Andrew's, Columbia College, the Chamber of Commerce, members of the bar, delegations of law students, and scores of distinguished citizens.[1] In front of the entrance to Trinity a platform had been erected, and here Gouverneur Morris delivered an oration, at the conclusion of which Hamilton's body was consigned with full military honors to the ground where Sir Henry Moore, Sir Danvers Osborne, James De Lancey, and others closely associated with Wall Street's history already slept, and where Robert Livingston, Marinus Willett, Morgan Lewis, and Robert Fulton were to find their final rest.

[1] The New York *Evening Post* and the New York *Commercial* of July 15, 1804.

XXV

THE LATEST PHASE

WITH this event the political history of the street may fairly be said to close, and during the next twenty-five years the new era, which had already dawned, slowly but surely developed. Close in the wake of the banks and insurance companies came the lawyers, and among the numerous representatives of the legal profession who established their offices on the highway about 1809 was a young attorney whose work was destined to give it a new and unique distinction. Washington Irving had originally studied law in the offices of Brockholst Livingston and Josiah Ogden Hoffman, two of the early practitioners in the famous Mayor's Court at the corner of Wall and Broad streets. In 1809, however, he was associated in practice with his brother John T. Irving at No. 3 Wall Street, and another brother, Dr. Peter Irving, had an office in the same building, and here it was that Washington Irving began the *Knickerbocker History of New York* which was to make him known to the whole English-speaking world.[1]

Meanwhile New York had scored another astonishing gain in population, for in 1810 the census showed no less than ninety-six thousand inhabitants, an increase of over fifty per cent. in the preceding ten years, and by 1820 the city included fully one hundred and twenty-three thousand souls.[2] Three years before this amazing result was achieved the brokers, who continued to assemble in steadily increasing numbers in Wall Street, organized under the name of the New York Stock and Exchange Board and adopted a written constitution, but they were soon driven from their customary haunt by an outbreak of yellow-fever, taking refuge for a time in Washington Hall, corner of Broadway and

[1] Washington Irving and Dr. Peter Irving were jointly responsible for the original idea, and they collaborated on the opening chapters, which were subsequently rewritten by Washington Irving alone.

[2] By 1830 population was approximately 202,000; by 1840, 312,000; by 1850, 515,000; by 1860, 805,000; by 1870, 942,000; by 1880, 1,200,000; by 1890, 1,500,000 (*U. S. Census Reports*).

Reade Street, but eventually finding their way back to the *Courier and Enquirer* building at No. 70 Wall Street, which sheltered them for a part of the decade closing in 1830.

By this time the street which had once been the centre of government and the resort of fashion had become completely transformed. Federal Hall, the wonder and admiration of the city, had disappeared, the buildings erected on its site had gone up in smoke and flames; the Bank of the United States occupied the present Assay Building; the great Merchants' Exchange, covering the block lately abandoned by the Custom-house, had been constructed, numbering among its many tenants the New York Stock and Exchange Board, and on all sides the hum of business was deepening into a roar. Old buildings were still giving way to new, however, and other changes were being effected, when the great fire of 1835 swept through the thoroughfare, levelling the monumental Merchants' Exchange and scores of other buildings to the ground; but almost before the ruins had cooled the work of tearing down and building up was resumed—and it has never ceased. "*It is as difficult to wend one's way*

WALL STREET DURING THE BANKING PERIOD, 1847–50

through Wall Street as it ever was," wrote the chronicler of the New York *Mirror* in 1839. "*Physically as well as financially there is peril in perambulating that street. Stocks may rise, but stones are falling prodigiously in all directions. The Manhattan and the City Bank are being torn down, and there are other edifices in old Wall Street under the besom. New York, ever since we knew it, has been a city of modern ruins — a perfect Balbeck of a day's growth and a day's dilapidation. The builder is abroad one day, and is relieved of his labors by the destroyer the day after. We never expect to see the city finished, but we have the greatest anxiety to see it fairly commenced.*"[1]

Almost threescore years and ten have passed since those lines were printed, but they fairly depict the modern conditions. Moreover, three years before the writer in the old *Mirror* described the physical aspect of the street, another contributor to the same periodical recorded some impressions of its life, which reflect the conditions of to-day.

"*Between ten and three o'clock,*" reports this observer of 1836, "*Wall Street is crowded with*

[1] New York *Mirror*, vol. xvi., p. 375.

speculators, money-changers, merchants, bank directors, cashiers, and a whole menagerie of bulls, bears, and lame ducks, and all is anxiety, worry, fretfulness, hurrying to and fro, wrinkled brows, eager eyes, calculating looks, restless gestures, and every indication which follows in the train of grim-visaged care. Wall Street is a place to study character, and the moralist would find material there to rewrite the 'Spectator,' the 'Tatler,' the 'Rambler,' and the 'Guardian,' with scenes, incidents, personages, and manners peculiar to New York, and to no other city under heaven." [1]

Such was the highway twelve months before its first great panic in 1837, and for the next three years the brokerage business languished to such an extent that the Stock and Exchange Board distributed its surplus among its members and virtually dissolved, though maintaining at least a nominal headquarters at one of the Jauncey buildings, No. 43 Wall Street. By 1842, however, the financial storm was over, and for the next twelve years the Board occupied a large hall over the reading-room of the new Merchants' Exchange, erected on the site of the

[1] New York *Mirror*, vol. xiv., p. 135.

building destroyed by the great fire, and so prosperous did it become during the interval that rivals[1] were induced to enter the field. During all this time the out-door market or place of public assembly for the brokers was on the corner of Wall and Hanover streets, but in 1854 the Board moved to the Corn Exchange Bank Building on the corner of William and Beaver streets, and from that day to this the Stock-Exchange has never, strictly speaking, had its headquarters on Wall Street. It would almost seem as though its change of base carried ill-luck, for one of the most notorious scandals associated with the history of banking and railroads in New York—the Schuyler frauds of 1854—occurred about the time of its migration, and shortly after it moved again to Lord's Court at William Street, Beaver Street, and Exchange Place, the great panic of 1857 caused wide-spread disaster and alarm. The full force of this financial convulsion was felt in Wall Street, for by this time the highway had become the banking centre of the metropolis, whose population had risen to

[1] It had at least one formidable rival prior to 1837, which the panic of that year virtually eliminated.

over half a million. Indeed, as early as 1850 there were no less than fourteen banks and sixty-nine insurance companies quartered on the thoroughfare,[1] and as the day of the modern office buildings with their thousands of tenants was still far distant, these concerns almost monopolized the limited territory. Every vestige of residential ownership had long since disappeared; the Presbyterian Church had been torn down and removed brick by brick to Jersey City; the Custom-house, occupying the former site of the City Hall at the Nassau Street corner, had been erected at an enormous cost; the street had been somewhat widened; the Trinity of 1790 had been demolished and the present structure erected, and other changes were occurring every year.

It was not until 1863, however, that the old Stock and Exchange Board became known as the New York Stock - Exchange,[2] and six more years elapsed before it merged its interests with those of its rival, the Open Board of Stock-

[1] From a rare publication of that year in possession of the New York Historical Society called *New York Pictorial Directory of Wall Street*.

[2] It moved into its present quarters, Nos. 10 and 12 Broad Street, December 9, 1865.

Brokers. Then came that Black Friday of September 24, 1869, well within the memory of many of its present denizens, when the street swarmed with demoralized victims and half-crazed captains of finance, while a little group of conspiring speculators dealt out ruin to thousands before they were themselves engulfed in the pit which they had digged.

From this time forward the history of the highway cannot be distinguished from that of the neighboring thoroughfares. Indeed, much which it is accused of and much that it is credited with is not properly associated with it at all, for the wide field of operations now conducted in its name is by no means limited to its own narrow confines, and "the street" no longer means the cañon down which Trinity gazes.

But though its story has lost in color and picturesqueness during the last hundred years, its fame within this period has almost reached the uttermost ends of the earth, and it would seem as though its latest phase, as the financial centre, was destined to endure.

Yet who can tell? The strip of land that has seen Stuyvesant's nine foot palisade rise to the gigantic walls of brick and stone which now enclose and shadow it—the spot where Zenger's words were burned and the Declaration of Independence read—the route along which royal pageants passed and the ragged Continentals made their triumphal march—the forum of the Revolution and the birthplace of the nation—the haunt of fashion and the heart of business—the home of Hamilton—the school of statesmen—the firing-line of commerce—the battleground of politics and of money—the scene of financial master-strokes and speculative orgies—of loud-tongued victories and wild-eyed panics—the lair of the money-spiders and the workshop of a Washington Irving and a Stedman—this is no mere street or thoroughfare. It is historic ground, of whose final destiny none dare prophesy.

WALL STREET IN 1908

CHRONOLOGICAL TABLE OF HISTORIC EVENTS IDENTIFIED WITH WALL STREET

1644. Governor Kieft erected cattle-guard near line of modern street (April 4th).

1653. Stuyvesant erected palisade on line of modern street (March–May).

1685. Street surveyed and established (December 16th).

1691. Captain William Kidd became a property holder (May 16th).

1696. Trinity Church erected.

1699. Stuyvesant's palisade removed.

1699. City Hall erected, corner of Wall and Nassau streets.

1702. Colonel Nicholas Bayard tried for high treason in City Hall.

1719. First Presbyterian church built.

1728. First New York library housed in street.

1734. Zenger's *Journal* burned at pillory (November 6th).

1735. Zenger's trial in City Hall (August 4th).

1765. Stamp-Act Congress assembled in City Hall (October 7th); petitions, memorials, etc., to King and Parliament draughted.

1765. Stamp-Act riots (November 1st–6th); stamps surrendered and lodged in City Hall.

1770. Statue of William Pitt erected, corner of Wall and William streets (September 7th).

1774. Mock reception to Captain Lockyer at Merchants' Coffee-house (April 22d), corner of Wall and Pearl streets.

1774. Committee of Correspondence appointed at Merchants' Coffee-house (May 14th).

1774. Paul Revere arrived with despatches from Boston (May 17th).

1774. Meeting of Committee of Fifty at Merchants' Coffee-house (May 19th).

1774. Answer of Committee of Fifty, suggesting Continental Congress, draughted at Merchants' Coffee-house, corner of Wall and Water streets (May 23d).

1775. News of the battle of Lexington received (April 23d); seizure of the City Hall by Sons of Liberty.

1775. Committee of One Hundred appointed in Merchants' Coffee-house to govern city.

1775. Marinus Willett seized arms (June 4th).

1776. Fortifications erected in Wall Street (April).

1776. Washington and Provincial Committee established headquarters in City Hall (April).

1776. Trinity Church invaded by armed mob (May).

1776. Declaration of Independence read from steps of City Hall (July 16th).

1776. Trinity destroyed by fire (September 21st).

1776. General Charles Lee a prisoner in City Hall.

1776–1783. Occupation by British troops.

1783. Triumphal entry of American troops; Washington banqueted at Simmons's Tavern, corner of Wall and Nassau streets (November 25th).

1783. Alexander Hamilton became a resident.

1784. James Duane, first American Mayor of New York, inaugurated at Simmons's Tavern.

1784. The Chamber of Commerce at Merchants' Coffee-house.

1784. Reception to Sir John Temple at City Hall (November 24th).

1784. Thomas Jefferson appointed minister to France at City Hall (March 10th).

1784. Bank of New York organized.

1784–1785. The Mayor's court opened on the corner of Wall and Broad streets.

1785. Celebration at City Hall on the first voyage of trading vessel from the United States to China (May).

1785. Continental Congress assembled in City Hall, corner of Wall and Nassau streets.

1787. Ordinance dedicating Northwest to freedom passed by Continental Congress (July 13) in City Hall.

1787–1788. "Federalist" papers written at No. 33 Wall Street.

1788. Demonstration on adoption of Constitution (July 26th).

1788. Corner-stone of Trinity laid; erection of Federal Hall begun by l'Enfant (August – September).

1789. Federal Hall, corner of Wall and Nassau streets, tendered to Congress of United States (May 3d).

1789. Canvass of electoral votes in Federal Hall resulting in election of Washington and Adams.

1789. Washington arrived at Murray's Wharf at foot of Wall Street (April 23d).

1789. Washington inaugurated in Federal Hall (April 30th).

1789. Senate, in Federal Hall, passed bill creating Supreme Court of the United States (June 12th).

1789. Washington, in Federal Hall, signed bill creating Supreme Court of the United States (September 24th).

1790. Trinity consecrated (March 25th).

1790. Petition presented to Congress for the abolition of slavery (February).

1790. Washington made last official visit to Wall Street (July 27th).

1791. Aaron Burr elected to the United States Senate in Federal Hall (January 3d).

1792. First "stock-exchange" opened at No. 22 Wall Street (March 1st).

1792. Stock-brokers first united for mutual protection (March 17th).

1793. Tontine Coffee-house erected, corner of Wall and Water streets.

1793. Franco-British riots.

1795. Governor John Jay inaugurated at City Hall (July 1st).

1795. Demonstrations against treaty with England; Hamilton stoned, corner of Wall and Broad streets (July).

1799. Manhattan Company obtained charter.

1804. Hamilton–Burr duel (July 11th).

1804. Hamilton's funeral (July 14th).

1809. Washington Irving became a resident.

1835. Merchants' Exchange and many other buildings destroyed by fire (December).

1846. Present Trinity Church completed.

1863. New York Stock-Exchange organized.

1869. Panic of "Black Friday" (September 24th).

INDEX

INDEX

INDEX

THE END

www.ingramcontent.com/pod-product-compliance
Lightning Source LLC
LaVergne TN
LVHW010554110826
845149LV00003B/660
9781418187606